Language
and Life

Reflections of a
Language Teacher

To the staff and students, past, present and future,
of Studio School, Cambridge

Language and Life

Reflections of a Language Teacher

P.R. Brown

DB
PUBLISHING

By the same author

Non-fiction:
The Gods of Our Time
Dreams and Illusions Revisited
The Mountain Dwellers

Fiction:
The Mirror Men
The Treadmillers
The Shadow People
Circle Walker
Diary of the Last Man
The Spare Room, Of Elves and Men
Undeliverable Letters, Unreachable Galaxies, or The Man in the Old Bowler Hat

First published 2024 by DB Publishing, an imprint of JMD Media Ltd,

Nottingham, United Kingdom.

Paperback ISBN 9781780916590

eBook ISBN 9781781563540

Printed in the UK

Contents

Introduction 9

1: Lexical Collocation: A Strategy for Advanced Learners 14

2: Role Play and Teacher Involvement 22

3: Teaching Punctuation 28

4: The Sound of Music 35

5: Pronunciation Theatre 39

6: Identifying the Discursive Conditional 46

7: Student Presentations:
Integrating Teaching and Studying 49

8: Confucius He Say: Responsibility for Learning 54

9: Tangential Self Development versus Neuro-Linguistic
Programming (NLP) 64

10: Tangential Self Development: The Flip Side 73

11: Popcorn Culture: The Use of Movies in Teaching 78

12: Political Correctness *versus* Common Sense 85

13: Language Patterns   101

14: Student Presentations: Technology in the Classroom   111

15: Teacher Motivation   119

16: Newspapers in the Classroom   127

17: Heaven Does Not Talk: Teacher Talking Time   136

18: Analytical Reading   146

19: Grammar Collocation and Sentence Structure   154

20: The Constraints of Dogma: The Dangers of Applying Inflexible Criteria in Teaching   163

21: 'Demand High'?: A Critical Postscript   176

22: Chess, Wardrobes and Pizza: Analogical Models   185

All the articles in this anthology are reproduced with the permission of Pavilion Publishing and Media

To say, as I have been tempted to say, that language *is* human life, is incorrect; but to say that language is a *part* of human life is a profound and widely misconceived understatement.

P.R. Brown

Introduction

This book consists of articles, published between 1994 and 2015, which deal with various aspects of the teaching of English as a foreign language. I have been persuaded to bring them together since they may be of interest not only to those who are teaching, working and studying in the field of Teaching English as a Foreign Language (TEFL), but also to those who have an interest, professionally or otherwise, in the practical business of language-teaching, in the teaching of English or indeed of any other language, for the themes discussed in these articles have application not only to TEFL but to language per se; moreover, it is essential to understand that the common denominator of these articles is what I call relationism, a term I have coined to distinguish it from relativism, as I shall explain below. Some of the articles are controversial and, I am told, original in their approach; be that as it may, my overall purpose is to engender some useful discussion on the matters dealt with.

Like many other fields of human endeavour, the teaching of English as a foreign language is subject to fashion and changing trends or, as I should prefer to call them, emphases; and as we all know, fashions come and fashions go; but what should be of enduring interest is the fact that students of the language wish to learn it, and teachers of the language wish to teach it. This fact, though glaringly and therefore humorously obvious when stated, is nevertheless worth fixing as our starting point for any discussion that may follow upon it, for, perhaps due to an excess of zeal for the latest fashion that happens to come along, mixed with a generous helping of gratuitous complexity and confusing jargon, it is one that may easily be forgotten. The articles were written over a span of twenty years. If nothing else, this collection can be said to represent an attempt to provide a personal validation of a lifetime spent in the teaching of English.

To grasp the general theme that runs through all these articles, it is essential to make a distinction between relativism and relationism.

Relativism

I am not a relativist. This is no place to enter upon academic philosophical discussions, especially in view of the fact that philosophical relativism is a house of many mansions in that it takes different forms, but a few highly simplistic observations of a non-academic or commonplace kind may perhaps be forgiven.

A relativist is generally thought of as one who believes that values and standards are *subjective*: things are different, but they are neither better nor worse than each other; there are no objective and absolute standards; whether, for example, a piece of music or a work of art is good or bad depends solely on how it is received; beauty is in the eye of the beholder; different tastes, not absolute standards, are the order of the day, so that whether or not a piece of music or of art is judged to be either good or bad is simply a matter of taste and therefore of subjectivity in that no appeal can be made to external standards to decide the matter either way.

I once made a squiggle on the whiteboard and asked the class whether it was art, perhaps even great art. I received only one reply, which was met with nods of approval here and there: 'Yes, why not? It all depends.' I was astonished to think that the speaker considered his clichéd response meaningful; to me it made no better sense than the meaningless squiggle I'd put on the whiteboard. I did not take the matter up; I lacked the energy; besides, a TEFL classroom was really no place for the labyrinthine entanglements of philosophical enquiry; I simply dropped the matter, hoping at least that the question I'd asked would linger in one or two minds a little longer, a catalyst for further thought.

(To repeat, this is no place for an academic discussion of different types of relativism, but for those who dare to enter the tortuous jungles of philosophical analysis, a more esoteric treatment of some forms of this persistent philosophical issue may be found elsewhere. See footnote 26 in Chapter 12.)

Relationism

I am not a relativist, which is perfectly consistent with the acknowledgment that *liking* or *disliking* something is indeed a question of personal taste. But, with certain caveats that will not be discussed here, I would not object to describing myself as a relationist.

Like the medicine men of the Lakota Sioux Plains Indians of Montana, who are given to concluding their religious ceremonies with the phrase 'mitakuye oyasin', I too believe that 'All things are related', or at least that *very many* things are related to one another and in ways that are most instructive. (I frequently have trouble with the word 'all', as I do with the word 'no'. Generalisation and simplification frequently charm us down perilous pathways which in turn lead us to inadequate, often dubious and sometimes absurd conclusions.)

The realisation that things stand in relation to one another, and frequently as cause stands to effect, has its drawbacks in the world of politics, religion and other forms of ferocious human activity: it can be extremely painful, irritating and frustrating to see how closely things are related, layer upon layer, like the layers of an onion but infinitely more complex to unravel and deep and dark like a philosophical conundrum.

But it can be very helpful, too. Take for example second-language acquisition. It is interesting, if not essential, to see how one piece of grammar is related to another ('grammar collocation') and how words are related to words ('lexical collocation'), and how words are related to grammar, grammar to words. Producing the wrong relations means using the language wrongly, which may give rise to serious misunderstanding or no understanding at all; using the right relations means using them correctly; and the more correctly they are used the better the command of the language in question.

I readily confess that I am not at all a fan of the suffix '-ism', but if we allow ourselves the extravagance of just one more '-ism' in a world which is already sadly over-burdened with them, we might say that 'relationism' encapsulates in one word a most useful insight into how the teaching and learning of a foreign language may be approached, not to mention the fact that our understanding of our own native language may be deepened and improved. Having before you the pieces of a vast jigsaw is an obviously important first step towards its completion, but if one fails to relate one piece to another it is hard to see how completion can ever be achieved.

Broadly speaking, this collection of articles is themed according to what I have called 'relationism'; indeed, the articles themselves are related, one to another. The stuff of language consists of language items in relation to one another.

But relationism takes us further. Language itself is related to the world in which we all live, the world of which it is itself a profound part, helping to make it the kind of world it is, enabling us to express relations between things, between people, between people and things. None of these relations would be the same without language. The world we see is the world we describe; and description is not possible without language. You may paint what you see, but without language you cannot describe what you paint. Language *per se* is the common denominator of our ability to describe and discuss each other and the world in which we live.

Suffice to say that this collection of articles is primarily and essentially concerned with (a) the relations we find within language, exemplified in English in this case, and (b) the fact that language, any and every language, relates to the world in which we all live.

To understand language is to understand the temptation to invent yet another '-ism' – relationism, and to give at least a nod in its direction is to understand the importance of language. Relationism, unlike many other '-isms', does not easily lend itself to dogma, for it simply suggests a useful *approach* to how language works as a living, breathing expression of life. If I were asked to coin a pithy phrase, the best I could come up with is: Language is life. It is *human life* at least. And herein lies the great importance we ought to attach to language teaching and language acquisition, whatever that language may be. 'Mitakuye oyasin' is a precept or 'sentiment' that came up in class when we were discussing Native American culture and heritage; we attempted pretty successfully to apply it to English, and the phrase stuck – I believe to very good effect.

P.R. Brown (Cambridge, 2024)

1

Lexical Collocation: A Strategy for Advanced Learners[1]

J ens Bahns, in 'Lexical Collocations: a contrastive view'[2] saw fit to pose a question that came close to giving me an irreversible cardiac arrest, namely: should we teach collocations? Either he was calling into question what I had been doing unquestioningly for the last 15 years, or he was presenting the phenomenon of lexical collocation almost as though it were a recent discovery which ought now to be given some credence in the practice of teaching English as a foreign language. True, his question was somewhat rhetorical, and he was drawing attention to the fact that collocation has until recently suffered comparative neglect. Nevertheless, I am bound to wonder whether I am in the minority in having given and in continuing to give a central focus to the presentation and teaching of collocation in the classroom, and I am prompted to outline the ways and means I have adopted to give it such centrality.

Strategy and motivation are two related notions that are conspicuously absent in the article in question. Tired teachers and tired students can

1   *Modern English Teacher*, Vol 3 No 2, 1994
2   Bahns, J., 'Lexical Collocations: a contrastive view', *English Language Teaching Journal*, Vol, 47/1, 1993

benefit from a framework of approach to the teaching and learning process. Placing emphasis upon lexical collocation provides such a framework. To appeal to lexical collocation is not to appeal to something recently discovered; one is simply getting students to look at words in a way new to them, new even in their own language. It is a kind of anamnesis, a 'recollection' of what they know already. Yet, although we appeal to what they already know, it often seems to them to be a new and exciting phenomenon; the newer it seems and the more exciting it is, the better, since what one wishes to achieve is a strategy that encourages motivation. Talk to them about the Collocation Experience:

'Birgit, suppose you're reading a page of German. You come to the end of the page, but not to the end of the sentence. But, just before you turn the page, you have an idea of what the next word should be. Are you right? Not always, perhaps. But when you are right, how is that possible? How is it possible for you even to think of the next word? ... And don't you have the same experience in French, Chantal? ... Yes, but do you have it in English? Can you guess the next word correctly? Do you have this experience when you read English? If not, why not? Have you ever thought about this?'

All students say they wish to learn 'more vocabulary'. But what this really amounts to is rarely explicitly addressed. Consider the following sentences in which students are asked to spot the error, and notice the words in italics:

The *crime* was done last night

The result was an extreme *disappointment*

Biochemists are making *research* into the causes of AIDS

We should do this *policy* as soon as possible

We'll experience many *costs* and few *benefits* will come

The concept 'advanced student' may be a house of many mansions, but most students classifiable as such will know the words in italics; indeed, it would be rather surprising if *any* of the above words were unknown. Moreover, the *proposition* expressed by each sentence is clear and unambiguous. From this we may deduce that the problem is not just one of words in isolation, nor is it an inability to communicate ideas. The problem is, of course, one of words in relation to words, that is, of lexical collocation: nouns in relation to verbs (crimes are *committed*, not *done*); nouns in relation to adjectives (disappointments are, amongst other things, *bitter*, not *extreme*). Almost any student of Business English, 'advanced' or not, will know the words 'costs' and 'benefits'; but few will know that costs are *incurred*, or that benefits *accrue*.

Students may be asked to play a word-game, rather like this:

Subject Verb Adjective Noun Preposition Object

Investigation

The idea is to surround the given noun with those linguistic elements that will constitute a collocationally correct sentence, e.g. 'The police are conducting a thorough *investigation* into the explosion', or 'The company is making a careful *investigation* into consumer complaints.' (Notice how we have some flexibility with noun and adjective, but not with preposition.) Again, the noun happens to be one which is already quite familiar to most students. The point is to help students to see that 'learning more vocabulary' is not simply a matter of learning new words (though it *might* be, e.g. 'incur' and 'accrue'), but of learning old words in (for them) new relations.

Now extend the game by listing 'research' under 'investigation'; does 'research' obey the same collocation rules? We 'conduct' investigations and we conduct 'research', but we 'make' investigations and we 'do' research. Such curiosities are noticeable; because they are noticeable, they are interesting; because they are interesting, they are motivating.

Students can be taught to read to see how words hang together. Here, as elsewhere, big things tend to come in small packages. Consider this extract quite randomly selected:

'It is easy to pay lip-service to the idea of equality for women, but in practice this is often difficult to achieve. People's attitudes do not change overnight, and it takes time, as well as education and example, to remove prejudice.'[3]

In a short space students learn that 'equality' is 'achieved', 'attitudes' can 'change', 'time' is 'taken' and 'prejudice' is 'removed'. (Lexical collocation is not of course all we learn from this extract.)

Students should be advised to read in manageable chunks, analysing sentences, noticing how words co-exist with others. And all this is part and parcel of teaching them to look not simply for new words, but at the words they know already; and not simply at the words they know already, but at these *in relation to* other words, many of which they will also know already.

Here, we are asking students to adopt a Green Cross Code of

---

3   Equality for Women – Sweden Shows How, International Business Topics, Unit 19, p.143

Reading: 'When you see a word, even, and in particular, a word with which you are already familiar (e.g. *investigation*), STOP, LOOK LEFT, LOOK RIGHT, LOOK LEFT AGAIN, AND, WHEN SATISFIED, PROCEED!' In a sentence like 'The police are now conducting a thorough investigation into the explosion', they should be satisfied when they have noticed and duly noted those collocational elements that make this an instance of the correct use of the word 'investigation'.

This is a reading strategy which is, for natural reasons, unnatural – because it seems much more natural to pause in our reading when we do not know the meaning of a word; we stop to look up an unfamiliar word in a dictionary, or to give it a dirty look, or to pretend it's not really there; we do not normally stop to take a wider look round a place that's already very familiar. Familiarity breeds contempt. But contempt gets in the way. After all, it might strike us that what seemed too familiar to be worthy of note is not all that familiar at all – in just the sense that every advanced student will know what 'investigation' *means* but will not know how to use the word with the correct collocation, i.e. will not know how to *use* it correctly. The reading strategy now recommended entails the refusal to take things for granted.

To help students to organise their strategy, Word Families can be constructed, each family consisting of words that can be grouped fairly loosely according to semantic similarity, e.g.:

A	B
Information	Part
Knowledge	Role
Wisdom	

Acumen

Experience

Skill

Talent

Intelligence

Worksheets can be made to illustrate the collocative requirements of each word in each family. Patterns may emerge. 'Part' and 'role' both take the same verbs and adjectives ('play' a 'part', 'play' a 'role'; both 'part' and 'role' are 'significant', 'vital', 'essential', peripheral', 'indispensable', 'leading'). If so, we may call them 'collocative synonyms'.

Which is the odd-man-out in **A**? 'Information', 'knowledge', 'wisdom', 'skill' and 'experience' are all 'acquired' and 'obtained'. 'Acumen', 'intelligence' and 'talent' are not. What verb would you choose to use with 'acumen' and 'intelligence'? Would 'develop' do? Questions concerning the correct collocation of a noun can therefore help to bring out its conceptual significance.

Emphasis on lexical collocation can even breathe some life into discussions of phrasal verbs. For example: we 'turn down' applications, opportunities, suggestions, recommendations, proposals, requests and invitations. We turn all these things down, or at least we do so in relatively informal English. But what about non-phrasal verbs? We 'reject' applications, suggestions, recommendations and proposals; we 'refuse' requests; we 'refuse' and 'decline' invitations; we 'ignore' opportunities.

If it is broadly correct to say that we tend to opt, where possible, for non-phrasal verbs in more formal English, we are now talking about *register*, or the social or task appropriateness of language. An exercise in lexical collocation becomes an inroad into social register. Which is to say, discussions of collocation are not a world apart from discussions of formality and informality. (What guides the choice between 'conduct' or 'make' with the word 'investigation', or that between 'conduct' and 'do' with 'research'?)

Talking about language *per se* may turn some people on; but the wise are interested in the world to which language relates. Pure Collocation is words in relation to words. Applied Collocation is words-in-relation-to-words in relation to issues like crime, pollution, war, education, poverty, homelessness, and so on. We might now tell students that they are playing chess in English. If they are talking about violent crime, it is appropriate to use words like 'deterrent', 'cause', 'punishment', 'policy', and so on. Appropriate words resemble pieces on a chessboard. The trick is how to move these pieces correctly. There are therefore two strands to the vocabulary game: choosing your piece (appropriateness), and moving it correctly (collocation). The selection of a discussion topic in the classroom is a means of motivating students to learn collocation; relations between swords still needs to be spelt out, but this is done in relation to the world in which we all live. In this way, language comes alive; it is indeed a living thing.

Emphasis on collocation is also a way to unlearn inhibiting preconceptions. Consider those students who imagine they discern the cold light of structure and form wherever they look and then seek to apply the logical 'must', a notion of stark necessity, even to a language other than their own. Present these poor misguided creatures with:

'The outcome was bitterly disappointing.' (Right)
'The outcome was a bitter disappointment.' (Right)
'The outcome was extremely disappointing.' (Right)

'The outcome was an extreme disappointment.' (Wrong)

Disappointments can indeed be 'bitter', but never 'extreme'. 'But how can this be so?' these students will ask themselves. 'Surely, what works for "bitter" must also work for "extreme"! Is it not a simple instance of mathematical transitivity?' Well, the rules of language are sometimes like those of mathematics, and sometimes most unlike.

It is not a question of belittling this type of student, but of trying to illustrate the sociology of language (any language), of bringing out the patterns where they may be discerned rather than of assuming that they can be constructed *a priori*.

Lexical collocation is not the alpha and the omega in the intriguing world of TEFL, but it is a creature whose tentacles are rightly irresistible. When people say that Cambridge is a good place to live, part of what they mean is that London is within easy reach, that airports are easily accessible, that you can get to other places with comparative ease. The focus that can be given to collocation is explicable in a similar vein. It seems perverse to undervalue the potential it offers as a means of accessibility to the multifarious uses of language. It is almost as perverse to speak of it as a relative newcomer which deserves a seat at table, though perhaps well below the salt of Grammar.

2

Role Play and Teacher Involvement[4]

Iwas particularly interested to read 'Teacher Role Play to attack Prejudice'[5] because the title is intriguingly ambiguous. The kind of prejudice Rinvolucri is talking about is cultural or moral, and student-centred. But implicit in the article is a challenge to a different kind of prejudice, namely that teachers ought not to get involved in role play at all, that teachers should not themselves play characters in the action. This is not a student prejudice, but a pedagogic prejudice, and is, it seems to me, worthy of note.

It is interesting how a change in circumstances may prompt us to question some apparently sensible assumptions. I recently felt obliged by circumstances to reconsider my views on teacher involvement in role play, and I am grateful for it.

In arranging role play I have at different times worked with at least three different models of teacher involvement, which I might classify as follows:

The fly-on-the-wall model, which is perhaps the most persistent and dominant model of all. Here my role is not to participate in the action of

4   *Modern English Teacher*, Vol 4 No 3, 1995
5   *Modern English Teacher*, Vol 2 No 4, 1995

the role play. I merely take up a monitoring position, ready to record the very good and the very bad. My role as guide and source of encouragement comes in before and after, in setting up and following up. But the role play itself is entirely the students' business – I've provided them with useful bits of language, and now I sit back and enjoy the fruits of my endeavours. After all, I don't want to be slapped down for excessive teacher talking (the dreaded TTT, Teacher Talking Time!). This is most appropriately called the fly-on-the-wall model, because teachers are so worried about being intrusive that they will not so much as cough for fear of upsetting the rhythm of events, the flow of discussion. 'Just forget I'm here,' I tell my students – reminding them of my presence in so doing!

The facilitator model, according to which the teacher not only feeds in before and follows up afterwards, but actually facilitates the role play by, for example, occasionally and discreetly handing prompts to various role players in the course of the role play itself. In terms of this model, it is important that I should not become too dominant, that facilitation should not become interference. It is therefore possible and legitimate to worry about over-facilitation. 'Is this really facilitation,' I ask myself, 'or am I forcing circumstances?'

The role player model, according to which I become one of the characters in the action: the teacher becomes actor. The difficulty here is that the notion of the teacher as role player seems to run counter to the eminently sensible assumptions which lie at the root of the fly-on-the-wall and the facilitator models. It seems to unjustifiably shift the focus away from the students, as if to suggest that they are being hard done by in not running the show entirely by themselves – as if by teacher participation I must mean teacher intrusion. The basic assumption here is that if

I become a role player, I am unable to discharge, or will discharge less effectively, the task of monitoring of facilitating. I will not be in a position to see the action of the group as a whole and will therefore be unable to monitor and facilitate 'properly'. Moreover, my participation will alter the 'group dynamic' – a delightfully vague phrase which suggests that students will perform differently and *therefore* less effectively.

What makes such assumptions appear unquestionable derives largely from the fact that we have seen fit to construct models in the first place – models which can, like all models, be taken too seriously. At best, each model suggests a different emphasis. Even so, I would go further and assert that it is quite possible to discharge, effectively and efficiently, the functions of monitor, facilitator and participator in a role play session. My confidence in making this assertion rests not merely on the results of practical experience. It stems also from the common-sense observation that participation does not exclude facilitation but is, on the contrary, a way of letting it happen or bringing it about. Teacher participation is itself a form of facilitation. Intelligent participation does not exclude monitoring, but in fact presupposes it; nor does it exclude the simple act of note-taking for future follow-up.

But models are hard to resist, for they tend to embody and encapsulate our prejudices: 'Yes, but even if I decide to participate, I couldn't be a key character, a strong character.' Why? Because then you'd hog the limelight? Even if you did, it might inject a valuable piece of realism into the proceedings. But as a teacher who is so keenly aware of the danger of teacher domination, you're less likely to overstep the mark.

Students get to know one another in role play; to that extent, role play is revelation, and the theatrical is only another dimension of reality and human relations. It follows that they will get to know more about you, and you more about them. There's nothing like playing a role to put you further into someone else's shoes. But it works the other way round, too: role play also tells us more about the shoes we ordinarily wear; which is why students enjoy teacher participation; they learn more about you as you become more vulnerable, a participator and not merely a judge. But isn't your participation linguistically off-putting? Isn't it inhibiting or a confidence-shaker? No, not necessarily. Let them hear bits of language they've forgotten or are still unsure about; if they trust you and feel sufficiently at ease, hearing you speak English will remind them, prompt them and even encourage them to imitate the models of language you are exemplifying. They will hear the language being used, as distinct from being talked about.

All of which is better, I believe, than a scenario which may seem intimidating to many, in which the teacher sits silently in a far corner of the room, like a watchful demon ready to record the forgetful, the unwary, the tired or the moody, only to pounce on them later and tell them what they neglected to say or do. True, it is useless to avoid one form of intimidation by adopting another; but again, intervention is not interference, participation is not intrusion. Where the one ends and the other begins is a matter of judgement, and bad judgement in this context is as likely or as unlikely as it is elsewhere.

If models are dangerous, so are irresponsible attacks upon them. There may well be occasions when one model is preferable wholesale to another, just as there are occasions when it is better for the teacher to take on a weak role, or play a strong role weakly. But the models I have outlined, while suggesting different emphases, also allow for different pedagogic functions to be performed in one and the same session. It is wrong therefore to understand these models as mutually exclusive. I was brought to an understanding of their compatibility by the force of circumstance: when I had eight good parts to allocate and only seven students to play them. Rather than ask a student to double up, or rather than discard the eighth part, I decided to become a thespian for an hour and a half. We all enjoyed it, and at points laughed our heads off. Did they actually practise some of the stuff I had taught them? Yes. Did they speak enough? Yes. Was I able to monitor and facilitate? Yes. Was I able to see how they functioned as a group? Yes. Was I able to correct errors of grammar structure, lexical collocation and pronunciation? Yes, merely by speaking English correctly! Was I able to write notes for follow-up? Yes. Did they derive more from it than the practice of some bits of language? Yes – some understanding of viewpoints other than their own – and perhaps something 'moral'. Did some cultural barriers begin to crack here and there? Yes, quite possibly.

In challenging the pedagogic prejudice that students should have exclusive territorial rights over the conduct of role play, both we and they might stand to gain. The theatrical monopoly we give to our students does not necessarily nourish them or fulfil them, and the fault sometimes lies with our slavish adherence to a simple model that we ourselves have ourselves constructed. We should loosen up in our thinking.

What about teacher participation in whole-class discussions, even in pair work? Sometimes I make up a group of three students when there is an odd number of students, which rules out all pairs, rather than taking part myself. Is that because I feel there is something intrinsically wrong in my forming one of a pair? Why must I feel like that? Why should I exclude myself? Admittedly, I am not the one who needs to practise speaking English, because my English is already fluent and accurate; but then, for this very reason, the student with whom I am paired is likely to benefit from the experience. So, am I working with a model that I tend to take too seriously? Why *must* it be a student who plays the part of chairperson in a discussion? Suppose no-one's up to the job; *must* one of them nevertheless give it a go? Is it always noble to 'give things a go'?

We should take care in our use of the word 'must'. A good teacher must not interfere. But this does not exclude intervention. And intervention might take the form of participation.

3

Teaching Punctuation[6]

The rules of punctuation vary between languages, so English punctuation needs to be taught as a constituent of good writing. In order to help our students in this potentially confusing area, there are a number of guidelines which we might do well to follow. What each of these guidelines suggests is that punctuation should never be treated as some tedious and purely academic abstraction from the use of the written language. Equally important, these guidelines show the *relations* between punctuation and words, punctuation and grammar structure, punctuation and sentence structure, punctuation and *sense*.

Punctuation patterns

We can teach punctuation patterns whenever possible. The word 'pattern' suggests something that is identifiable and repeatable and therefore imitable. Students can be taught to identify and imitate a 'punctuation pattern'. Such patterns may be simple or increasingly complex.

a) The colon as an explanation signal

I was exhausted: I had spent all night travelling in a stuffy train without anything to eat or drink.

Charles I was executed in January, 1649: he had been tried by a people's court and found guilty of High Treason, a charge which he had earlier dismissed as illogical.

John Merrick (the Elephant Man) was not a pretty sight: his forehead and the right side of his face were so hideously deformed that he had to wear a large bag over his head.

b) The semi-colon in the role of full stop

She was a highly competent teacher; moreover, she seemed to have a way with children.

Environmental pollution is a very serious problem; however, no steps have yet been taken to combat it effectively.

It is important to reach a decision soon; on the other hand, we should take care to make the right kind of decision.

c) The colon as an explanation signal and the semi-colon as full stop

Custer's decision was disastrous: he had ignored the advice of his scouts and had consulted no-one; however, there is some evidence to suggest that he himself thought that his luck was finally running out.

d) The colon as explanation signal and the semi-colon as replacement comma

Retail outlets may be large or small: the supermarket, which deals mainly in foodstuff; the department store, usually dealing in clothes and durables; the smaller stores, specialising in footwear or quality clothing; and the traditional 'corner shop', a typically one-man business.

Punctuation and words

We should not forget that punctuation and words are related. There are, for example, a host of phrases which require a comma after them when they begin a sentence, and commas before and after them when they are used within a sentence. Such words and phrases include sentence adverbs, sometimes called sentence-linking devices. Words and phrases like *generally speaking, in my view, according to* ... should be presented with their punctuation requirements.

The punctuation patterns in b) above should be taught together with sentence-linking devices like *moreover, however, on the other hand.* Here, the patterns are: ; *moreover,* ; *however,* ; *on the other hand.*

Semantic similarities between sentence-linking devices should, whenever possible, be presented hand in hand with punctuation patterns. For example:

Group 1

Though he was tired, he continued working.

Even though he was tired, he continued working.

Despite the fact that he was tired, he continued working.

In spite of the fact that he was tired, he continued working.

Regardless of the fact that he was tired, he continued working.

In this group, the sentence-linking devices follow the punctuation pattern of conditional, or *if*, sentences. When the if-clause (the *condition*) comes first, it is followed by a comma to separate it from the *result* (or main clause); when the result comes first, the comma is omitted: *He continued working though he was tired.*

Group 2

He was tired. Even so, he continued working.

He was tired. However, he continued working.

He was tired. Nevertheless, he continued working.

In Group 2, the full stop could be replaced by a semi-colon (a comma would not suffice): *He was tired; even so, he continued working.*

The occurrence of such patterns should not be treated as incidental to such sentence-linking devices but as part and parcel of their correct use in written English – in particular more formal or academic written English. Different punctuation patterns are also intrinsic to *different uses* of such sentence-linking devices – for example, where the linking device does not begin a sentence but is contained within it with the use of commas as parenthesis:

Group 3

He was tired. He continued, even so, to work.

He was tired. He continued, however, to work.

He was tired. He continued, nevertheless, to work.

(Notice the anomaly in Group 3, where stylistic preference seems to require the full infinitive after the linking device instead of the gerund.)

Semantic differences between sentence-linking devices may not necessitate any change in punctuation patterns. For example, while all the linking devices in all the above groups are *contrastive*, non-contrastive links like *moreover, in addition, furthermore* follow the same punctuation patterns as those in Groups 2 and 3 above.

Contextualisation

While relations between punctuation and words should not be overlooked, punctuation should really be presented in full context, and, wherever possible, the context provided should aim at a topic of general interest, perhaps a topic the class is currently discussing. Students can then understand the role of punctuation more clearly, and more pleasantly; punctuation should seem much less of a confused and confusing abstraction. When reading a text they can more easily recognise legitimate uses of various punctuation marks and imitate these in pieces of extended writing of their own; the point here being that the correct use of punctuation is a requirement of acceptable sentence structure.

Function

Connected with the presentation and teaching of punctuation in relation to words and context is the functional use of punctuation: in narrative, discursive and, say, formal letter writing. Some instances of function have already been given: the sentences chosen to exemplify punctuation patterns and punctuation-in-context may illustrate a variety of different functional uses.

The general point is to give the learning of punctuation *sense* by illustrating *use*. On the question of sense, we might note that the inclusion or exclusion of punctuation can dictate the sense of a word; for example, when 'however' is used as an adverb of degree as distinct from a sentence adverb:

However hard he tried, he couldn't start the engine.
He was dead tired. However, he continued working.

In a) the absence of a comma after 'however' indicates that it is an adverb of degree; its inclusion in b) indicates that it is a sentence adverb.
Function and sense must obviously go hand in hand. Social register comes into the picture here. Consider the difference between:

'There's a lot to say – anyway, I'll be in touch'. (informal text, email, letter)
'There is more to discuss; however, I look forward to our next seminar.' (formal)

The punctuation in a) is arguably one of the ingredients of informal English.

And finally...

Students sometimes ask how long a good written sentence should be. Perhaps if discussing the sad history of Native Americans and the fateful Battle of the Little Bighorn, students can be asked to say how many sentences there are in this piece of highly perspicuous English, to help them understand that a sentence can be as long as good punctuation allows:

'In concluding to go into camp for a brief period on the banks of the Arkansas, two important objects were in view: first, to devote the time to refitting, reorganizing and renovating generally that portion of the command which was destined to continue active operations during the inclement weather season; second, to defer our movement against the hostile tribes until the last traces of the fall season had disappeared, and winter in all its bitter force should be upon us. We had crossed weapons with the Indians time and again during the mild summer months, when the rich verdure of the valleys served as bountiful and inexhaustible granaries in supplying forage to their ponies, and the immense herds of buffalo and other varieties of game roaming undisturbed over the Plains supplied all the food that was necessary to subsist the war parties, and at the same time to allow their villages to move freely from point to point; and the experience of both officers and men went to prove that in attempting to fight Indians in the summer season we were yielding to them the advantages of climate and supplies – we were meeting them on ground of their own selection, and at a time when every natural circumstance controlling the result of a campaign was wholly in their favor; and as a just consequence, the troops, in nearly all contests with the red men, had come off second best.'[7]

Whether his career was glorious or vainglorious, 'General' George Armstrong Custer was capable of impressive lucidity, with the minimum of editorial assistance!

---

[7]   *My Life on the Plains*, G.A. Custer

4

The Sound of Music[8]

Music is pretty generally used nowadays as a form of listening comprehension, which usually means some kind of gap-filling exercise. There is nothing wrong with the regular gap-filling exercise; long may it continue. But music, by which I mean both songs and instrumentals, has other uses, and I am moved to reflect on the uses to which I myself put it. I use it habitually, even to the extent that I have become the butt of jokes like 'If you want to know where he is, just follow the music', or 'He must be in room 17, because that's where the music's coming from'.

For one thing, music, of almost any sort, may be used as a starter to lessons, and it is especially welcome as a palliative to those Monday Morning Blues. Why be in a hurry to start the lesson? Why not spend a few minutes listening to the music, instead? Music can help create a welcoming atmosphere while at the same time signalling a start to the day. Similarly, it can be used at or near the end of a lesson, to signal that it is time to wind down or to stop. I tend to use it both at the beginning and the end of lessons, both as a signal, and because it creates a pleasing atmosphere.

---

8   *Modern English Teacher*, Vol 7, No 3, 1998

Background music can be played during lessons, particularly when the class is engaged in some kind of writing or grammar exercise. It seems to soak up any peripheral or wandering concentration, so that students can actually focus better on the exercises they are doing. Here, soft music is obviously preferable to heavy metal. Music doesn't form the background to every lesson; but it often does, and not merely unintrusively, but helpfully.

One of the most important functions of music in the classroom is that it can help students to *relate* to one another; and teachers to relate to students, and vice versa. Students can be invited to play their own music preferences and explain them; teachers can engage in the discussion and describe their own preferences. In this way, students and teachers learn more about each other, while in the process they are practising both their speaking and listening skills and testing out appropriate descriptive lexis and employing the language of preference. They can also prepare their own listening exercises on the lyrics of their favourite songs and conduct the exercises themselves with the rest of the class – an excellent recipe for student-centred lessons, with the teacher functioning as a resource of last resort. In this way, students are participating in the process of teaching, which becomes part of the process of learning.

Music, perhaps with some exceptions, is no doubt the food of love, as indeed love, with similar exceptions, is the food of music. But it is also the food of thought and conversation. It is, after all, a universal conversation piece. It can therefore generate a great deal of discussion, sometimes heated, not necessarily in any organised or systematic way, but in the more general run of communicating likes and dislikes, in the course of getting to know more about other people, and indeed oneself. Talking about music preferences can be a good way of breaking the ice. More elaborately, it can form the basis of more extended language projects, under such headings as 'The Contribution of the Beatles to Music', 'Social Themes in Tracy Chapman', and 'The Poetry of Bob Dylan' – the more controversial the topic, the more useful and fruitful it is in the production and practice of language! And even if the student's or the teacher's preference is far from mainstream, like, for example, early music, it can still be listened to and discussed: 'Listen to this and tell me what you think about it? Can you identify any of the instruments? Can you imagine people listening to this or dancing to this? What kind of people do you think they were? Would it be right to say that music has *progressed* since then? Is music now more *advanced*, more *civilised*, even? Is this kind of music *primitive*, or is it too *simple*, or is it wrong to think in this way?' The point here, of course, is that even from an unlikely beginning, a great deal of vocabulary and other lexical items can be generated and practised ('It's not for me', 'It doesn't appeal to me', 'I don't find it appealing', 'It's not my cup of tea', 'I wouldn't call this *music*! ...).

Similarly, since music has to do with expressions of feeling, there is ample scope for discussions about the feelings expressed by this or that piece of music, and therefore golden opportunities to talk about and use the language of emotion. Few people dislike all kinds of music (with the exception, allegedly, of Quentin Crisp). This means that we have a subject that should be more profitably exploited in the classroom – because it is so close to people's feelings, memories, hopes. If discussion means communication, and if communication tends to close gaps as well as open them, then there is another kind of gap-filling exercise that music can be instrumental in helping to close, namely the cultural gap, and also the generation gap, both amongst students and between teachers and their students. We should invite students from different cultures to present the typical or traditional music of their own countries, to see what the reaction is; for the reaction is also the practice of the target language. Music tends to break down barriers rather than fortify them; it can bring very different people together without at the same time dissolving those differences, just as students might laugh at the same (English) joke without abandoning their national identities.

Music can help teachers, too. It can play a role in combating the stresses and strains of their chosen career. Music is often used in the home to unwind, so why not use it for the same purpose in the classroom? Why not play a familiar piece or song? Familiarity may sometimes breed contempt; but it may also relieve tension, for both teachers and students alike. That is another worthy topic for class discussion: stress and how to beat it. Music has a multiplicity of social and psychological functions; it is therefore a catalyst for discussion in the classroom. Music can therefore not only help to make teaching more effective but also more enjoyable, by bringing us closer to our students, and perhaps more importantly, closer to ourselves; after all, if teaching ceases to be enjoyable, then Heaven help both teachers and students alike!

For me, music is not now part of an occasional lesson (e.g. as a random gap-filling exercise), nor is it merely an occasional indulgence (e.g. because Christmas is here and it's time to play some carols). It has become a daily occurrence and something which my students have come to expect and even to relish. Occasionally there is a dissenting voice, largely because this or that student has never previously experienced music in the classroom, and it seems to them out of place; exclamations of shock and horror are never ignored, but they are extremely rare. In the main, students love the sound of music and benefit enormously from it.

5

Pronunciation Theatre[9]

Aspects of what we collectively call 'pronunciation' (subject-verb contractions, intonation, syllable stress, intonation patterns, rhythm, weak forms, phonemes and diphthongs) are no doubt each deserving of a separate focus as part of a gradual initiation into how English is spoken by native speakers; it is a vital part of an analysis and explication of how English sounds as it does. And practice in each aspect in the form of drills of various kinds no doubt has its place, as do recognition exercises in the form of games, many of which consist in some form of sound-matching.

That said, and despite some ingenious attempts by some authors to arouse interest, I have yet to find exercises and drills of this sort which satisfactorily engage learners and make the learning and practice of pronunciation a truly *meaningful* enterprise and one to which learners can more easily *relate*. And it is not simply learners who fail to be absorbed in the process. Teachers themselves generally find little to attract them to the whole business of getting their students to understand and practise the elements of pronunciation. The reason, I suggest, is that such drills and exercises all too often fail to provide realistic contexts for pronunciation,

---

9   *Modern English Teacher*, Vol 8, No 1, 1999

contexts in which the various elements of pronunciation can be seen to hang together in the expression of something meaningful, particularly in the expression of feeling and human relations.

What is needed is to find a way of illustrating how these elements are related and to bring them to life in functional contexts to which learners can more easily relate. Generally, these contexts will have to do with the communication, not so much of ideas in themselves, but of moods, feelings, and attitudes in such functions as persuading, reprimanding, the expression of interest, disappointment, anger, frustration – and a host of other moods, attitudes and feelings to which learners, as human beings having much in common with others of the same species, cannot help but relate. The presentation and practice of pronunciation in such contexts is a more direct and enjoyable method of enabling learners to see how and why English sounds as it does.

An exercise in listening comprehension, for example, might consist in getting learners to listen to a monologue or dialogue and to offer a description of the kind of people talking, a description based not merely on *what* is said but on *how* it is said: they are invited to give a character and personality description of speakers and of speakers' feelings based on intonation, word stress, speed of delivery, and so on. While all learners say that they want to improve their pronunciation, the extent to which they will do so depends not merely on how much they practise, but also on their ability to imitate the sounds and sound patterns they hear as exemplars. (It is not simply a question of practice, if only because it is always possible to practise the *wrong* way of doing things!)

In my own teaching, I introduce the element of theatre into the presentation and practice of pronunciation. *Dramatic Monologues for*

Listening Comprehension, by Colin Mortimer, is in this respect a collection of exercises brought together under a misleading title, for these exercises are eminently usable for pronunciation practice in conjunction with listening practice, since listening obviously provides the models for subsequent practice. Indeed, it is hard to see how many of the questions relating to these exercises can be answered correctly without an understanding of the elements of pronunciation with which they are expressed! Listening comprehension and the understanding of how feelings are expressed are therefore inextricably linked: it is not simply the words *per se* that are spoken, but *how* they are spoken that needs to be taken into account. In the Introduction, Mortimer says: 'Though they are scripted, the monologues simulate many of the characteristics of natural spoken English.' But it is just for this reason that these monologues are excellent sources of pronunciation practice. Any example chosen would amply illustrate how the elements of pronunciation combine in the expression combine in the communication of moods, feelings and attitudes. Consider the woman who is irate after things have gone wrong at the hairdresser's:

'I **know** there's nothing I can do about it. Of **course** he can't put it back again! But at least surely I have the right to let off steam a bit, don't I? I mean, I **told** him, didn't I? I **told** him! Just a bit here, I said. Just a little bit here, and just the tiniest bit there. And nothing at all off here. Nothing. Well, then I closed my eyes, as I always do. That's part of the satisfaction, I always think – it's, well, it's relaxing. But he kept on snipping and snipping and suddenly I came out of my daydream and looked in the mirror. Ugh! Well, I told him what I thought of him, I can tell you. I mean, if it'd been my first time, it would've been different. But I've been going for months, and it's always been perfect. Anyway, never again! And don't try to tell me it's not too bad, because it's terrible – you **know** it is. Look at it! Just look at it! You can smile if you like, but I'll tell you one thing: we're not going this evening – or at least **I'm** not going. I can just see their faces if I did. I can see your **sister's** face, especially. Anyway, they'd prefer to have you on your own. And you know what I think of your mother's cooking. Tell them I've got a cold. Well, I soon **will** have, won't I?' (Monologue 5)

Ask students what they can say about the person speaking – first about her immediate feelings, and then about the kind of person she might be. What can they say about her relationship with her in-laws, and with her husband for that matter. Is it just her hairdo that's the problem – or is it something deeper and wider than that? These questions will go together with an analysis of some of the elements of pronunciation: question tags, subject-verb contractions, word stress and intonation patterns expressive of anger, irritability and frustration; (note also the contractions in the type 3 conditional sentence). Questions about her mood and even the kind of person she may be are in this way bound up with an analysis of some of the typical elements of pronunciation; pronunciation ceases to be a mere abstraction and becomes a window into real life and real people; we are reminded that language is the outcome of human relations and is inseparable from them.

Having listened, more than once and at their own pace, to the original monologue, students can then practise it themselves – either as a sort of 'talking' head or to a partner. If the partner is her husband, what are his physical responses likely to be – his facial expressions, his gestures, if any; what might he say? Is he dismissive, or is he wimpish and therefore silent in cases he puts a foot wrong and brings down even greater wrath upon himself? There is much fun to be had in this whole exercise – but at the same time, the situation is real enough and neither the speaker nor her husband are rarities in the real world, and we may ask whether theirs is a marriage made in heaven or one which is merely the product of long and unhappy habit. There is depth as well as amusement here. The main point of the whole exercise is to show that pronunciation is intrinsic both to the amusement and to the depth, so that the understanding and practice of pronunciation is given a context in real life, something to which learners can more readily relate.

Learners need to be involved in the language they are learning, and the elements of histrionics already referred to can be extended into small theatre. *The Play's The Thing* (book plus cassettes) is an old BBC publication consisting of one-act plays, each about eight minutes long and acted by professional actors. Once again, the actors provide the models which students can subsequently imitate. The exercise can be done as a play reading, or, more ambitiously and time-permitting, students can learn their parts by heart. There is, I would suggest, nothing so effective in the improvement of pronunciation than participation in a play – nothing so 'involving'. Here the elements of pronunciation are brought together in the portrayal of characters – of moods, feelings, reactions, attitudes. Plays need to be rehearsed; this is where the real fun comes in, but rehearsals also ensure abundant pronunciation practice. Moreover, teachers as well as students participate in what is being learned and practised; the teacher now functions as director, as much concerned with the personalities behind, as it were, the sounds the characters make as with the sounds themselves (e.g. does the intonation correctly express the personality/character of the speaker?). In fact, it is not now sensible to distinguish between the character and the sounds the character makes – and therein lies the point and the interest in the sounds, since these sounds are not now 'entities in their own right', but intrinsic to an understanding of people, of what interests people, what worries them, what makes them 'tick'. The study and practice of pronunciation is therefore once again given a point.

Using the term 'drama' somewhat loosely, any monologue or dialogue can function as pronunciation theatre. *People Talking*, another BBC publication, is copiously illustrative of the elements of pronunciation in the expression of feelings and attitudes. It consists of interviews with or about famous people: e.g. A.S. Neill, Kim Philby, Arthur Hailey, Christopher Lee (Dracula). Although the principal purpose of this collection is to test listening comprehension, students can act out the interviews, imitating their 'dramatic' elements, e.g. imitating the interest shown by a speaker in the subject he is talking about, and reproducing intonation patterns, word stress, and so on. Consider the word stresses in Patrick Seale's description of Kim Philby:

> 'He was a great **bureaucrat**, he had a first-class **intelligence**, and he also had **considerable moral arrogance**; I think he felt he was **right** all along; and he also had – I think we must give it to him – **considerable courage**. He wasn't a man **built** for taking great risks, he wasn't **physically** very strong, which makes in a sense the life he chose to pursue, the life he was **forced** to pursue, all the more **taxing**.'

There is much more here, too: the great speed of Seale's delivery, for example, suggests his interest in the subject – as though he's worried about getting it all in before he runs out of time. He speaks quickly, and the fact that he stresses some words serves to underline his interest in or his commitment to the subject he is addressing. But correct word stress implies correct syllable stress if the words stressed are not to sound ludicrous, and this helps us to indicate to learners the importance we must attach to stressing the correct syllable in multisyllabic words in the communication of feelings and attitudes. What we can tell about Patrick Seale is that he is intensely interested in what he is talking about; this is bound up with the stress he gives to *ideas* or *concepts*, and this in turn is connected with correct syllable stress in the words which express them. The study of syllable stress patterns therefore gives a sense, a point outside itself, a sense or a point that is most certainly in the real world of people and human relations.

The texts I have referred to have been those I know and which are for me readily accessible. There is of course an abundance of published material more or less usable in the ways I have suggested, apart from what we as teachers can ourselves put together for our own purposes. By appealing to the theatrical in our students, we are appealing to what is invariably of interest to them, which is why we rarely find students who have no interest at all in cinema. If we now say that the theatrical is an imitation of life, and if the ability to imitate is an important factor in the improvement of pronunciation, then we seem to be presented with a more fruitful approach to both the presentation and practice of the elements of pronunciation.

References:

Mortimer, C. (1980) *Dramatic Monologues for Listening Comprehension*, CUP

BBC English Courses, *The Play's The Thing*

Owen, R. (1976) *People Talking*, BBC

6

Identifying the Discursive Conditional[10]

T he failure to relate grammar structures more closely to the real-life contexts in which they occur may be responsible for the fact that a structure worthy of mention which we may call 'the discursive conditional' is left out of account in presentations of conditional sentence structures.

The classification of conditional sentences into types 0, 1, 2, and 3, has a pretty wide currency. However, many non-if sentences are also translatable in terms of this classification. 'Go on like this and you'll come to a sticky end' is recognisable as type 1, while 'One false move and we'd have fallen to our deaths' is translatable as type 3. Sentences that are not strictly conditional may nevertheless be fruitfully compared with sentences that are: 'As soon as I get there, I'll give you a call' is structurally comparable, though not semantically identical, with 'If I get there, I'll give you a call'.

It is wrong to say that this classification is not truly or accurately representative of what is to be found in the language, since it is an extrapolation from what is found there. Nor would it be right to underestimate its importance in the classroom, both as an instrument in the way in which structures are first presented and as a useful reminder

10   *Modern English Teacher*, Vol 8, No 4, 1999

when the structural going gets tougher. The classification is an organiser in the business of learning about a complex organism, namely language.

However, although it is an accurate extrapolation, we should not forget those contexts in real life from which it is derived. This reminder is all the more crucial when we acknowledge that the classification is not exhaustive. For instance, in the context of discussion, we often encounter a structural cocktail which I call the discursive conditional. This is found often enough when speakers or writers wish to emphasise the idea of necessary connection between condition and result. Sentences of the form 'If we are to reduce the crime rate, we must address the root causes of crime' consist of the present simple of the verb *to be* + full infinitive, in the condition, and *present modal* + infinitive without *to* in the result, are not immediately recognisable in terms of the standard classification of types into 0-3; they are certainly not straightforwardly compatible with that classification. If we add passive constructions and invert condition and result ('The root causes of crime must be addressed if the crime rate is to be reduced') and, although we have a form which is common enough, it is one that may well boggle the minds of learners and throw the traditional classification into some disrepute.

True, no classification can sensibly claim to allow for every conceivable structural permutation, but I am struck by the fact that grammars and course books consistently fail even to identify this common variant. The discussion of environmental pollution, to name but one topic in which a suitable context might be found, could amply demonstrate the life and sense of this particular structural creature: 'If the planet is to be inhabitable for future generations, urgent steps must be taken to deal with the problem of global warming'. Appropriate contexts for the presentation of grammar are infinitely preferable to a mere classification followed by an exercise; exercises of this kind have their place but must be denied exclusivity; exercises and context must, whenever possible, go hand in hand.

7

Student Presentations: Integrating Teaching and Studying[11]

Granted the desirability of maximising the degree of student involvement in the process of study while at the same time not making teachers utterly redundant, and given that this is a means of improving student motivation such that involvement and motivation are related rather like cause to effect, and given, further, that there is such a phenomenon as over-dependence on course books and that such dependence is demotivating for both teachers and students alike by frequently obviating the need for creativity and risk-taking, it would seem that current trends are likely to be liberating.

The trend towards the further study of English to satisfy the language entry requirements of UK universities shows no sign of abating. On the contrary, the recent expansion of the European Union and the continued interest shown, notably, by the Chinese market in, especially, commerce, engineering, human resource management and medicine, provides new scope for old opportunities in the classroom. Naturally, such trends apart, the nurturing of study skills and their integration can be no bad thing; but the whole phenomenon has now acquired new impetus and point, and the case for it is worthy of restatement.

Consider student presentations. Students can be asked to choose a topic to talk about and present to the class; the idea is that they should choose topics which interest them, on the assumption that this criterion of choice will maximise their involvement and their motivation and that, in so doing, the end-product presentation has a fair chance of engaging the attention of the audience, too.

In terms of current trends, the ability to conduct presentations bears relation to the ability to participate effectively in seminars; and the ability to function effectively in seminars presupposes a high level of competence in all the language skills. The structured preparation and conduct of presentations provides the teacher with a degree of specificity in the teaching syllabus, but one which is not related to an amorphous entity called 'a class', but to individuals *within* the group. The teaching, which is of course still directed at the group, is nevertheless instrumental in helping individual students to achieve a satisfactory end-product, namely a competent presentation. Each end-product is the brain-child of the student, while the process towards that end-product is presided over by the teacher.

To put some flesh on these bare bones, the process of preparing presentations can be divided into three phases:

Phase one: topic selection

Research: reading and listening

Understanding headlines, headings, subheadings

Understanding key lexis, key words, idiom

Understanding gist, grasping main points

Understanding supporting examples

Understanding overall organisation: sentence and paragraph linking

Phase two

Ordering material and ideas; writing

Accurate note-taking

Converting notes into sentences

Organising sentences into paragraphs

Use of ordering devices, 'signposts', linking devices

Overall organisation

Having something to say; critical thinking and arguing cases

Agreeing without plagiarising

Phase three

The presentation: speaking, listening

Use of presentation aids (whiteboards, overhead projectors, etc.)

Clarity and pace; pronunciation

Structuring the presentation, giving it clear shape and direction

Inviting and answering questions, dealing with criticism

Clarifying points and examples

Helping to conduct discussion

Parallel teaching

The elements which constitute each phase in the process towards preparing presentations form the features of a workable teaching syllabus, thus ensuring relevant teacher input in ways designed to help students express their own ideas. *What* they say is their own business, but *how* they say it should comply with recognisable standards if what they say is to be effective. The process towards helping them to effective self-expression may be called 'parallel teaching'.

Peer assessment

Part of the litmus test of effectiveness is not simply how the teacher sees it but how the student's peers see it. Peer assessments of effectiveness should be encouraged, fostering a spirit of teamwork and cooperative learning. If the presentation is viewed as a mini-lecture, listeners can practise their note-taking skills, which presupposes listening comprehension for gist and for detail. In the question session which follows the presentation, students practise their ability not simply to ask questions, but to ask questions which are relevant and meaningful, and in ways which are constructive, so that questions can further discussion and not stifle it, and so that errors or omissions in the presentation can be corrected, for the presentation can be regarded as work in progress.

Listeners can be given a simple checklist to record their impressions as to how they think the presentation went, and these can then be discussed, e.g. they can rate the following 1-10:

Presentation structure:

Pronunciation:

Vocabulary:

Grammar:

Treatment of questions:

Use of presentation aids:

Naturally, this is properly workable only if we assume a sufficient degree of maturity and amiability on the part of the class. This degree of involvement and participation in the process of learning ought to help students to relate better to one another and to their teachers; it also *presupposes* that there is already a satisfactory rapport. But whether or not it is in the particular case sufficiently workable, peer assessment does not of course exclude teacher assessment; assessments from both sources should aim at complementarity and parity, since the teacher is as much on the receiving end of a presentation as peer listeners, while peer listeners should themselves aim at the standards set by their teachers.

8

Confucius He Say: Responsibility for Learning[12]

I read with much interest the piece entitled *Preventing Stress and Burn Out*[13]. The author seeks to give practical advice, and what is said is perfectly valid and helpful, as far as it goes. I do not wish to dispute, merely to pursue. The issue I should like to discuss is 'expectations'. How much can be expected of the teacher, and how much they can expect of themselves.

William James, the American psychologist, had much to say about education that is of enormous universal and practical relevance to teachers and students alike. He wrote most of his stuff before the turn of the 19th century, and it is most suggestive that his analysis and remarks are as relevant now as they were then, if not more so. He referred to the development of what he called 'soft pedagogics': 'We have of late been hearing much of the philosophy of tenderness in education; "interest" must be assiduously awakened in everything, difficulties must be smoothed away. Soft pedagogics have taken the place of the old steep and rocky path to learning. But from this lukewarm air the bracing oxygen of effort

---

12   *Modern English Teacher*, Vol 14, No 4, 2005
13   Linda Bawcom, 'Preventing Stress and Burn-out', *Modern English Teacher*, Vol 14, No 2, 2005

is left out. It is nonsense to suppose that every step in education can be interesting.'[14] It is just as true to say that not everything can be easy.

It is interesting that there is such a thing as the 'development of soft pedagogics', for developments in education, as indeed elsewhere, are highly suggestive of *trends*. And trends, I regret to say, are seldom regarded as useful emphases and general correctives to be taken for what they are; they more often enjoy the status of dogma, and then they get us into all sorts of difficulties. Trends require a little wisdom for their interpretation and application, and wisdom never was and never will be in superabundance. So, the problem with 'soft pedagogics' is that we poor pedagogs, vulnerable creatures that we are, are in danger of developing a conscience whenever we are confronted with blank faces which we then automatically interpret as a vote of no confidence in our lesson materials, or in our abilities as teachers, or, perish the thought, in ourselves as persons. Not everything can be interesting.

Which is why the question of how much we can reasonably expect of ourselves as teachers is connected with how much we as teachers can reasonably expect of our students. Few teachers, for example, would, in the normal run of things, confront their students with a long list of phrasal verbs first thing on a Monday morning (or first thing on any morning, come to that). This is not to say that it cannot be done, or cannot legitimately be done. It is only to say that it is not normally wisely or caringly done. Whenever it is done, conscientious teachers would contextualise the items in question in the most interesting or amusing reading passages they can find or devise, stretching their poor imaginations to the utmost in the interests of their students. Teachers do this because they are conscientious

---

14   William James, *Talks to Teachers*, Geo. Ellis, Boston, 1899

and sufficiently caring to realise that a mere list of phrasal verbs in and by itself is of limited interest. The fault, if 'fault' we call it, is not with the teacher but with the subject matter. Personally, I am surprised to encounter any smiling face on a typical Monday morning, taking the sea of indifference as a signal that 'serious' or 'boring' stuff may be welcome later, but not just yet. I might invite students to ask one another 'Monday Morning Questions' (about their weekend activities) and postpone 'teaching' until I feel the time is right. (But in serving them, I also serve myself.)

Such are the concessions we make to the frailties of human nature. But such concessions must come to an end, and efforts must be made. This is the 'bracing oxygen' of William James. And have we forgotten that what you can expect to get out of a thing depends on what you are prepared to put in? As conscientious teachers we should certainly do what we can to create interest and to utilise the interest that already exists, principally by contextualising the language we teach in the real world from which, after all, it comes and to which it relates. This is what we should do, but it is also what we do with varying degrees of success. Teachers can get things wrong, but if we all see in a glass darkly, we should at least be given some credit for striving to see at all.

Motivating students can be hard work, and what helps to keep me going is the realisation that I cannot do everything, that I should not therefore try to do everything, and that I cannot achieve the same degree of success with everyone at one and the same time. There are degrees of success, partly because the people I teach are different, sometimes very different. Some students may be bored with English because they are bored with everything. Goodness help us! What is to be done when an 'inner life' comes across an 'inner vacuity'? The best we can do is the best we can do – to show interest in what we are teaching and hope that some of that enthusiasm will rub off. And teachers need to be many things: advisers, psychoanalysts, social workers, friends. A qualification in TEFL is not the only requirement of good teaching, or, at least, it isn't if we put humanity first. But I also realise that students, too, have their responsibilities as learners and that teaching is not a one-way process; if it were, students would be deprived of much that is invigorating and challenging about the whole business of learning.

'Soft pedagogics' are not only a recipe for teacher stress, anxiety and self-doubt; they are also a surefire way of lessening a student's joy of discovery, of independent thinking and hence self-development, of the satisfaction of having worked something out, or of having pursued something until it 'clicks'. True, 'soft pedagogics' has done us the service of humanising education by being a corrective to sheer brutality, insensitivity and crudity. It has done enormous service; but as a dogma it is a recipe for boredom and lassitude on the part of students (the attitude being that if a thing doesn't have them poised on the edge of their seats, it isn't worth knowing), and destructive self-doubt and disillusionment on the part of teachers (the belief being, if I'm not a first-class entertainer, I'm a third-class teacher).

Mr James is dead. But he has much to teach the living. Taking liberties with language, I should like to point out that the Chinese teacher Confucius is even deader. In about 500 BC he is alleged to have said, 'Only one who bursts with eagerness do I instruct; only one who bubbles with excitement do I enlighten. If I hold up one corner and a man cannot come back to me with the other three, I do not continue the lesson'[15], the point being that Confucius 'had little patience with the dullard and the lazy, insisting that a student must

---

15   *Analects*, 7:8, Waley's translation

not only be eager to learn but willing to cooperate with his teacher by giving earnest application to the subject'[16]. Oh, what impossible luxury! – to be able to say: 'Well, since nobody seems to be interested, I'm not going on. Lessons are cancelled. So, bye-bye, we'll try again tomorrow, maybe.' Such was the contempt Confucius showed for laziness, and such was his insistence that a student must not only be ready to learn but also willing to cooperate with his teacher by giving earnest application to the subject above and beyond a mere going through the motions. But such, too, was his confidence: confidence in the relevance and importance of the subject matter, and his self-confidence, his conviction that he was able to do the job. In his remarks about laziness, Confucius was not only commending student conscientiousness; he was also giving credit to the subject-matter and to himself.

We are not very good at giving ourselves credit, and we should be far better. Instead of self-confidence, we are bedevilled by self-doubt; instead of confidence in our subject matter, we often appear to be apologetic – 'I'm very sorry I have to teach you some phrasal verbs, but, you see …' Well, then, why don't we apologise for teaching English at all and be done with it? And it may even be a short step from here to apologising for our very existence. We are in danger of apologising ourselves away into the ether.

I rather suspect that what James called 'soft pedagogics' is the cause or the outcome, or both, of our inability to give ourselves and our profession sufficient credit. Confucius and James were not merely good analysts; they were exceptionally good teachers; perhaps there is a connection here; in any case, they were far too wise to be taken in by dogma.

Both James and Confucius understood that a teacher is rather like a psychoanalyst in that neither can get very far without the whole-hearted

---

16   D. Howard Smith, *Confucius*, Granada Publishing Ltd., 1974

cooperation of student and patient. How does the psychoanalyst know he has provided the correct analysis? When the patient says 'Yes, that's how it is' and feels unburdened. How does the teacher know that he has got places? When the student can produce what he has been taught, as the tree is said to be judged by its fruit. Cooperation and effort are prerequisites; patients cannot be cured by force; and students can't learn merely by attending class.

In fact, Confucius has done us the invaluable service of reminding us that laziness does in fact exist and is not simply a vicious fabrication of some monstrous Mr Gradgrind which was finally put paid to thanks to right-minded people like Mr Charles Dickens. (For a moment there, I felt pangs of conscience, as though I should never use the word 'laziness', which must have been expunged from the dictionary at just about the same time 'soft pedagogics' was invented, like a dishonoured General drummed out of the army he himself helped form.)

From the fact that conscientious teachers are always striving to be better, it does not follow that they are not good, and perhaps exceptionally good, already. From the fact that good teachers should endeavour to excite the interest of their students in the subject matter, it does not follow that students themselves have nothing whatever to do but sit back and be excited. (In fact, excitement can never come to those who simply wait for it, limp and immoveable.) Learning implies responsibility on the part of learners, and, as we all know, at least in our heart of hearts, a sense of responsibility is not given to all. There are limits to what teachers can achieve, whatever boundaries they succeed in pushing back. There are therefore limits to what they can sensibly expect of themselves. They should not succumb to bouts of depression and self-doubt as though these demons were simply part of their job description.

Teachers are in the very business of trying to make second-language acquisition interesting and relevant. They teach bits of language by relating them to the real world of physical geography and social issues; they do their best to make courses relevant to examinations, and their teaching in general relevant to personal or professional aspirations. All this they have done and continue to do, and for the most part admirably.

But consider the bogey of lesson-preparation. James offered this advice, 'Prepare yourself so well in your subject that it should always be on tap' so that you can 'trust your spontaneity and fling away further care.'[17] This is music to our ears. It deserves to be read with the utmost care, because 'trusting your spontaneity' means, if it means anything, 'feeling OK with yourself'. In general and ideally, no lesson plan, no teaching method, no course book, no worksheet, should be permitted to stifle the personality of the teacher; if it does, it should be consigned to the flames. It is the personality of the teacher that students should be invited to know; if the teacher feels ill at ease with a lesson plan, teaching method, course book, or worksheet, these 'helps' should be amended or replaced or dispensed with altogether. It is through the personality of the teacher that students come to know the language. A teacher teaches his students about himself before he teaches anything else. If this sounds too bizarre to be palatable, it is only another way of saying that it is the person of the teacher that makes it possible to get the very best out of the material he uses, with the corollary that if the personality of the teacher is 'mechanical' and off-putting to his students, they will fail to get the best out of the material or methodology on offer.

---

17   William James, *Talks to Teachers*, Geo. Ellis, Boston, 1899

But why is preparation a bogey? Because good preparation is a first principle of good teaching, and 'first principles' tend to become *fixations* for conscientious teachers, who are often given the spur by teacher training manuals and overzealous teacher trainers, in much the same way that trends tend to become dogma; and fixations and dogma are frightening things when they are not simply unhelpful. Preparation is a prop of teaching, but even good props can never compensate for poor acting; and good preparation can never compensate for poor teaching. To teach well, you must, at some point and in some way, have prepared beforehand, even if you never actually wrote anything down on paper and your teaching is 'spontaneous'; but you must also be yourself, and you cannot be yourself if you rely too heavily on material that you have meticulously prepared in advance and for the occasion, as though the material is capable of speaking for itself, interpreting itself and able to meet by itself everything foreseeable and unforeseeable. Teaching without personality is like a marriage without warmth.

The simple but vital truth is that the majority of us tend to over-prepare, and too much preparation is stifling. We prepare too much, because we feel insecure. We feel insecure, because a natural pre-requisite poses itself as a dogma to which we 'must' adhere on pain of inability or incompetence. Like good musicians, we recognise the need to tune our instruments to perfection; like absent-minded musicians, we tend to forget that the strings have been tightened well enough already. PING! Unable to let go ourselves, having already achieved optimum tuning, our beloved instrument does it for us with a broken string; in teaching, with the unfortunate result that the lesson went badly. Some teachers take more than one lesson into the classroom, like so many insurances; and while an insurance policy is a wise thing, if you buy too many of them, you won't have enough cash left to survive. The tendency to overdo it, to leave no stone unturned, no contingency unplanned for, can also be seen in the extraordinary world of course books, where some writers cram so much between the covers that you might be forgiven for thinking that they are attempting to bring about early retirement for teachers *en masse*.

We should try to be more ourselves, and then we shall do a better job. But we look into a mirror and see a reverse-image. We try (too hard!) to do a better job, and then we are less ourselves. William James once used the image of a bicycle-chain that is too tight, making cycling less than a pleasurable experience. Insecurity is burdensome; it shows in our teaching, because it shows everywhere. Teaching EFL is a fascinating and worthwhile occupation. To get the very best out of it requires us to be human first, teachers second. Dogma and the insecurity it fosters reverses this. To say that the job is fascinating and worthwhile is not to say that it is easy, but insecurity is a burden which increases the weight of every other, and we can do without it.

I still believe what I believed long ago, that successful teaching requires a kind of moral courage. For example, it takes courage to leave the troubles of one's life at the door and enter the classroom smiling and receptive to the problems of others. To those that say the job cannot be done in any other way, I would reply that it cannot be done *well* in any other way. Nor is it simply a question of wanting to hold on to one's job solely for its pecuniary benefits – because this is cynical, synthetic and unconvincing. It also takes moral courage to be as nearly yourself as you can be, to be transparent without loss of self-esteem, guileless but at the same time discreet, willing to admit error and ignorance without blushing, ready to accept peccadilloes but also to stand firm against the unacceptable, able to maintain a sense of humour without loss of stature, and generally having the courage of one's convictions and the ability to call yourself stupid in public. A prerequisite of moral courage is confidence in yourself and in what you believe and do.

Perhaps it is also a kind of moral courage to give credit where credit is due when this credit is due to yourself. Sometimes, students more easily give credit to their teachers than teachers tend to give to themselves. Modesty may forbid it, but many teachers are reluctant to give themselves credit for the work they do. This may simply indicate how conscientious they are; but stress, anxiety and self-doubt may be attributed to many truths or half-truths masquerading as dogma, and such dogmas may make us reluctant to acknowledge the credit due to us. Our students dine well on the diet we provide. Are we not to be given the crumbs that fall from the table? We cannot live happily for long on a one-sided diet of 'soft pedagogics' and muddled dogma.

9

Tangential Self Development versus Neuro-Linguistic Programming (NLP)[18]

'The discussion of the application of Neuro-Linguistic Programming techniques to EFL raises fundamentally important questions about what teaching EFL is and about teacher-student relations. While such a discussion may be invaluable, it is also true that certain approaches to NLP may be off-putting and misleading, and that an overzealous appreciation of the merits of NLP may serve to undervalue what was done before NLP was "invented" and what is in any case often ordinarily done.'

In what follows, I respond to Mario Rinvolucri's invitation[19] to *MET* readers to send in their own thoughts about NLP and EFL 'and thus initiate a debate around this important new (and not so new) area in EFL thinking'. I must assume amongst readers a general idea of what NLP is all about, but at the end I list two relatively lucid websites that readers might like to visit.

---

18   *Modern English Teacher*, Vol 15, No 3, 2006
19   *MET*, Vol 14, No 4, 2005

The phrase 'new, and not so new' is at least mildly suggestive. By discussing in what sense this area is new and in what sense it is *not* new, we might begin to discover what it is about it that is objectionable and what it is about it that is unobjectionable, respectively. Rinvolucri believes that some aspects of NLP would not go down well with people from 'Confucian cultures, such as China and Japan' since in such cultures value is attached to collectivism and group achievement, while NLP focuses on individual potential and individual achievement. This I believe to be a false, and *importantly* false, dichotomy. However, I shall not challenge it here. Here, my misgivings are not at all Oriental.

First, and in general, a debate on this whole issue is invaluable in that it raises questions that are fundamental concerning what EFL is, and, in particular, how teachers go about teaching it, how they perceive their role vis-a-vis their students, and, more generally, how teachers believe they stand in relation to life and the world in which they find themselves.

I do not believe that a teacher's role in TEFL either can be or should be confined to the bare teaching of bits of language and all that goes with them (grammar, lexis, pronunciation, and all their subsets) in any way unrelated to the real world to which it all applies and from which it derives any sense it has. This 'real world' comprises people and human relationships of all kinds (love, friendship, marriage…), sociopolitical events, and the vast array of problems that human beings in ways complex and simple create for each other. If I may be forgiven for quoting myself, I long ago stressed what we all know, namely the importance of relating *lexical collocation* to the 'real world': 'Talking about language *per se* may turn some people on; but the wise are interested in the world to which language relates. Pure collocation is words in relation to words. Applied collocation is words-in-relation-to-words in relation to topics like crime, pollution, war, education, and so on'[20].

But what an NLP focus in EFL helps us to remember is that the 'and so on' in the above quotation includes us, both teachers and students, as *subjects* of our own questioning. If (as I try, though not always successfully, to believe) an unexamined life is not worth living, the whole phenomenon of questioning applies to us as the subjects of our own questions. Such questioning implies self-analysis, self-criticism, a desire to question our own beliefs, attitudes, prejudices, our patterns of thought and behaviour. The connection with language *per se* is logically fundamental: questioning of *any* kind makes no sense without language, if only because sense derives from language and not vice versa. But the connection between NLP and *my* use of language is equally obvious: what I say and how I say it reveals a great deal about my thought and behaviour patterns, attitudes, beliefs, etc. If this is what NLP helps us to remember, such reminders may be important and useful, but they merely *articulate* what we know already. It is what teachers already know and what underpins what they do and have done all along when they relate language and bits of language to what we might call 'the real world'. Once again: 'There is no new thing under the sun, saith the Preacher.'

Critical self-analysis and self-awareness is what NLP is all about, if it is about anything at all, but not, of course, for their own sakes, but with a view to self-development or self-growth. A kind of personal and moral teleology is thought to be involved here. The notion of a moral teleology may be understood in this context as the idea of helping someone to achieve their full potential, to abandon fruitless negativity and achieve

---

20   *MET*, Vol 3, No 2, 1994

their personal goals and, in short, a happier life – and all this seems perfectly respectable. (In fact, statements like these, despite their apparent respectability, almost invariably bristle with difficulties, but for reasons of space and strict relevance, they must pass muster here; we must take them as read, as most people in fact do.)

However, in *explicitly* using English as a tool in helping our students towards self-development, and *explicitly* using ourselves as teachers in the role of facilitators in the whole process, the focus on NLP tends to come across to many as so much mumbo-jumbo and quackery. If not sheer impertinence. To put it another way, as teachers we might appear now to be *exceeding our brief*, which is to teach the language 'pure and simple'. Personally, I do not think that NLP is mumbo-jumbo or quackery; still less do I think that there is, ever was or ever will be, such a thing as 'teaching English *pure and simple*', if that phrase means anything at all. But the problem is one of perception, of how things are viewed. How things are perceived is vital. If you have no faith in your GP, you are hardly likely to follow his prescription and will seek advice elsewhere, or nowhere at all if your distrust is universal. It is precisely winning the confidence of his patient that should be the first and greatest task faced by the analyst or therapist.

It is this *explicit* focus that is new in TEFL, one which gives it a doctrinaire feel. And it may not be doing itself many favours in consequence. Which is why I would advocate a more *tangential* approach. And this now brings us to matters that are as old as the hills in any teaching that is worthy of the name. For there is an infinity of ways in which good and mindful teachers can help set the stage for the self-development of their students, and, for that matter, for their own self-development. (Were we to dig deep enough, we might begin to see that the self-development of teachers and that of students are closely linked, and sometimes inextricably.) One example must suffice.

Consider the importance of critical questioning in the context of classroom discussions of familiar classroom topics (love, crime, poverty, capital punishment, friendship…). A discussion, if genuine and free, is a way of discovering not simply what others think, and hence what kind of people they are, or think they are; it is also a good way of discovering more about yourself, of the kind of person you are, or think you are; and the interaction between these discoveries provides an excellent opportunity for self-questioning and self-development, though the fruits of the process may not appear until a long time later – you might defend a position tooth and claw, but then go away and think about it, and turn it upside down.

Self-discovery through interaction with others and the observation of others is not at all new. As R.L. Stevenson so aptly put it: 'If you want to know yourself, study others; if you want to know others, study yourself.' The phenomenon of self-discovery through interaction and discussion is common enough, and for that reason can be expected to take place in the classroom, whether or not it is acknowledged by participants. Self-discovery involves self-questioning. This kind of questioning has in common with all other kinds of questioning that it seeks answers; but it is unlike many others in that it is *self*-directed; it is therefore a kind of questioning that seems at best inappropriate and at worst idiotic in mathematics, physics or chemistry.

It is platitude that the best teachers seek to bring out the best in their students, but there is surely much more to this than the achievement of high grades or the best academic or professional recommendations, yet all this is supposed to be the essence of our *brief* as TEFL teachers. So much for remaining within our brief! If this is a debate about the point of teaching, it is similar to that about the point of education. If such debates are to have any depth at all, they are about values and an old-fashioned belief in 'the meaning of life' having to do with the pursuit of truth, which includes the truth about ourselves, and happiness – a belief which, though it now goes on crutches, still tags along somewhere in the background. In any case, this belief is not simply about how to produce engineers, doctors and IT whiz kids, however important such professions may be.

Insofar as NLP in connection with TEFL seeks to assert the importance of the opportunities presented through L2 language acquisition of self-questioning, self-discovery and self-growth, it is unobjectionable; it is even commendable in that such reminders can never possibly be untimely. For this reason academic jabbering about the necessity of 'testing hypotheses' is NLP is to achieve respectability misses the point and does so monumentally; thus Rinvolucri is right to dismiss those academics who reject NLP as being an unproven set of hypotheses (*ibid*); they might just as well say that the truth of the proposition 'Oxygen is necessary for living organisms' has yet to be demonstrated.

Which is not to say, however, that NLP should be *argued* monumentally in public when that public is our students. An instrument might have a vital role to play in an orchestra, but played too loudly it is apt to produce a discordant note and precipitate a mass exodus, while those who remain in the auditorium are likely to be labelled either tone-deaf or helplessly eccentric. Sometimes the most important notes must be played with great delicacy if they are to be heard at all, let alone appreciated.

And so we turn full circle to *problems of perception*. One problem with NLP is not with its essence but with its presentation, not with the gift but with the packaging. The teacher-student relationship tends to be seen as therapist-patient, the teacher playing the role of the all-knowing therapist, and the student seen as the recipient of his kind though sometimes painful offices. Intelligent people are rightly sceptical of anything that poses itself as an all-embracing insight into a better world beyond, just as they are asked to be sceptical of that proverbial pot of gold at the end of the rainbow. They may then go on to say that those who claim benefits from the methods of NLP are simply subject to the placebo effect. Quite simply, people resist what they doubt, even if this means that the greater the resistance the greater the need for the methods of NLP – and so the circle spins and we are caught up in its vortex. NLP is making a rod for its own back simply in calling itself 'NLP' and by presenting itself (or being presented) as a set of inalienable doctrines fresh from the treasury of human discovery and understanding. No wonder some academics approach it so critically, and so *wrongly*, for academics like nothing better than to set fire to men of straw. True, the therapy analogy has its uses. Which is why it should be retained. But it is also off-putting. Which is why it should be scrapped. In philosophical discussions, Ludwig Wittgenstein would sometimes say 'How can I remove this disease?' when criticising a way of thinking about a philosophical issue. He had a point in calling it a 'disease', though one that was seldom appreciated. People whom reject a gift on account of its packaging are in danger of rejecting the gift as well, as the baby is said to be thrown out with the bathwater.

Perhaps it is better to encourage self-questioning and self-development while appearing to strive for something else – for example, the practice of relevant lexis, in a classroom discussion of the value of education! Sometimes the best things are achieved tangentially, and sometimes this is the only way the best things can possibly be achieved. Tolstoy is supposed to have said that a good writer should turn his back on his readers (and he should know!).

Good teachers having been doing the same things since teaching began, plying their art without at the same time elevating it to doctrinal status, edging their students, explicitly or implicitly, towards self-questioning while appearing to be teaching such banal, unexciting stuff as verb declensions and syntax, gerunds and phrasal verbs, quadratic equations and Boyle's Law. What is good about NLP in relation to TEFL is good because it refers to something that has stood the test of time, namely that good teachers are human first, teachers second. Which is why it may seem to some as though NLP is attempting to teach wise old birds how to suck eggs.

The best possible compliment a student can give a TEFL teacher is something like this: 'Thank you for teaching me, not just English, but about life and myself.' Rare? Yes, but you would expect the best possible compliments to be so. His teacher taught him English, of course; but *in such a way* that his student could teach *himself* the rest.

The emphasis on NLP *per se* can at least be irritating, because it comes across as doctrinaire and is not anchored in real context. Which is why perhaps some of us may feel somewhat uncomfortable with Rinvolucri's NLP-inspired questions for students; not because we have some deep-seated emotional hang-ups and stand in dire need of a heavy dose of NLP, but simply because they are dry and unapproachable:

'How do I feel when I think about starting something new?'
'What are my feelings half-way through a journey, a task, a project?'

But starting *what?* you feel like asking. *Which* journey? *What* task? *What* project? And *where*, and *when*, and what *kind* of...?

Such questions seem abstract and as relevant as algebra. We climb a vertical rock face with no hand holes, and with no relief in sight even for those of us who do miraculously get to the top, though the top of what, and for what purpose we climb, remain obscure, largely because such questions or prompts are not contextualised and therefore hard to relate to. After all, such questions are not self-authenticating. What about: 'How do I feel when faced with questions like these?'

Useful websites:

www.nlp-now.co.uk/nlp-what.htm

www.businessballs.com/nlpneuro-linguisticprogramming.htm

10

Tangential Self Development:
The Flip Side[21]

What follows is a postscript to 'Tangential Self-Development versus NLP'[22], which focused on the role of teachers in student 'self-development'. The point I wanted to express there is perhaps expressible in an aphorism we can invent for the occasion: 'Good teachers teach, great teachers educate.' In other words, there is more to teaching than the mere transmission of bare facts, and too much clamour surrounding the phenomenon of NLP is likely to disguise the fact that the truth expressed in this aphorism has stood the long test of time. Crudely put, the focus so far has been on what teachers can do for students.

If we now change this focus, and ask what students can do for teachers, we may find that there is a kind of reciprocity here, such that, in helping students towards self-development, teachers are in fact doing much to make their own self-development possible.

First, we must question our terms. 'Self-development' is a word that has become fashionable in many areas of life, and, like many other bits of jargon, its meaning is not immediately clear. The fact that such terms

21   *Modern English Teacher*, Vol 16, No 1, 2007
22   *MET*, Vol 15, No 3

are rarely understood but nevertheless bandied about as though they were perfectly acceptable currency, only goes to show how far one can get in many walks of life merely by unquestioningly adopting the jumbled notions of one's contemporaries. No doubt the term 'self-development' may mean very different things to many different people and is therefore a house of many mansions. For want of space and motivation, we can at least try to settle on a common denominator. So, whatever it means, the term is likely to suggest the notion of *enrichment*, perhaps in one's intellectual or moral understanding or appreciation or clarification of some aspect of life or person, including of course oneself – though 'knowing oneself' is, as philosophers through the ages would readily admit, an onerous task that is often not even embarked upon, let alone completed. But the intellectual or moral understanding, appreciation or clarification involved has, presumably, little to do with improving one's understanding of phrasal verbs or this or that grammar structure. But what about the word 'self'? Surely the word is not meant to imply that the kind of development we are talking about can take place 'by itself', or that my 'self-development' is something I can achieve, as it were, by myself, as if to suggest that it is achievable in a kind of *vacuum*. Can *anything* take place in a vacuum? Hardly.

But why? Because growth requires oxygen, and the oxygen of my growth is *other people*. Self-development takes place, if indeed it takes place at all, *through* others, not without them or despite them – through my *interaction* with what they *say*, what they *write*, how they *behave*. The engine of self-development is motivated, inspired, characterised, given substance and direction in and through my dealings with other people. It is, as it were, a *response* to others. It is in any case *grounded* in others. For example, genuine self-development, like genuine discussion, demands that we are good listeners first, critics second. We listen to others, what they say and write, and we observe how they behave.

Since students are 'others', it would seem to follow that they might have much to 'teach' their teachers, even if they can seldom be credited with the *intention* of doing so. They teach despite themselves, if, that is, their teachers are good listeners, that is, good students, and good students are sufficiently open-minded to learn. What students teach in this way may not always be original, or vastly illuminating, or even palatable. We must not make the mistake of thinking that self-development must always be a *pleasant* experience; for it may involve the abandonment of previously held assumptions which were, though wrong, comforting. But the point is that interacting with students, listening to them, engaging with them, are the conditions without which a teacher's own self-development, *qua* teacher, would not be possible; though, naturally, the circle of the brethren may be widened, for a teacher interacts with his *colleagues* as well, and can learn from them what to do or what not to do. Is not all this simply a restatement of a well-documented truth, that 'No man is an island unto himself'? Yes, it's an old tune; but if an old tune is worth playing, it's worth playing more than once.

But the level of abstraction here is likely to make us all a little light-headed. We need to put some flesh on these bare bones by asking what it is that students can possibly teach their teachers if insights into such stuff as English lexis and verb tenses are rules out of court. This is not to say, of course, that teachers cannot enrich their understanding of the language they teach in the course of teaching it, in response to the difficulties students face, or indeed the insights that a student may indeed have.

Many readers may perhaps recall one of the many memorable scenes in David Lynch's *The Elephant Man* in which John Merrick (The Elephant Man) thanks his doctor, Frederick Treves, for all that he has done for him. Treves replies: 'Yes, well, you've done a lot for me, as well.' Treves, as Lynch paints him, is just too good a man to mean by this that Merrick has helped him to further his career by boosting his reputation as eminent physician, although this is probably very true. Now can he mean that now he, Treves, has discovered the cause and cure of Merrick's medical condition, multiple neurofibromatosis, for these were not known and are not known now. So just what has Merrick done for Treves? It is perhaps doubtful whether Treves himself could have given either an immediate or very clear answer to this question. But if we were to try and put one into his mouth, it would probably have to do with some kind of *enrichment* of Treves's life, some difference in his understanding of the trials and tribulations of life and of how some people try to face up to them, or of some kind of 'inner beauty' that somehow manages to survive despite appalling odds or that emerges and grows *because* of them, of some values that distinguish man from brute, values that define the best of what man is or could ever aspire to be. In the classroom, a discussion of the movie *The Elephant Man* can help to clarify such insights, and there is no reason to assume that they must emanate solely from the teacher; the teacher has no monopoly over moral insights; students are just as capable; and the sights that the movie reveals to students might be an important aspect of their own self-development; both teacher and student may in this way be enriched from the messages the movie may be said to contain.

Some kind of enrichment is bound up with self-development, and it may of course be little more than a better understanding of the requirements, refinements, benefits and drawbacks of one's own choice of career, and so a better idea of where one stands in relation to it. Whatever it amounts to, whatever its nuances in the particular case, it is the very best that a teacher can expect in and from his dealings with others, where those 'others' happen here to be his students. It is of course *tangential*: unexpected, unforced, not made to order. It does require an openness towards others, and so it requires teachers to be human before they are anything else, and human-*ness* in plenty is a prerequisite of an educator as distinct from a teacher. Which is why a machine may one day replace teachers but never *educators*. It is hard to embrace any worthwhile notion of self-development that does not require sensitivity and receptivity as its preconditions – and such virtues are aspects of genuine humanity.

No student joins a class expecting to teach the teacher anything. The fact that he may yet do so points to what it may mean to say that the best teaching is more than (is *other than*) the mere transmission of bare facts. So self-development for teachers is akin to self-development for students; they are linked by a natural reciprocity the conditions of which are a willingness to learn and an unattachment to mere cant and dogma.

11

Popcorn Culture: The Use of Movies in Teaching[23]

How can movies be used in the classroom? They may be used as a form of relaxation, as pure entertainment, with no particular language purpose in mind, and, indeed, as a means of getting away from the whole business of learning and being taught. Far be it from me to decry this. Doing nothing, or nothing in particular, and doing it usefully, is a skill to be envied and cultivated. And at this level of interest the movie really need not be in English at all, not even subtitled in English! A bit of slapstick would amply fit the bill, or our friend Mr Bean would do very nicely. Just in case TEFL fans of Mr Bean may be reading this, I hasten to add that the wordless Mr Bean can be very useful for teaching purposes: putting words into his mouth, predicting his next move, or simply narrating the story or describing the situation, expressing opinions, and discussing different kinds of humour. But then, Mr Bean would not be watched purely and simply to 'get away from it all'!

The use of movies in the world of TEFL is often rationalised in terms of topic or theme, because movies can obviously help to exemplify and

23   *Modern English Teacher*, Vol 16, No 3, 200

develop the topic under discussion elsewhere in the timetable. Examples are naturally plentiful: *The Day After Tomorrow* (global warming, the natural environment); *The Nutty Professor* (junk food, obesity, obsession, personal relationships); *All Quiet on the Western Front* (the insanity of war); *The Elephant Man* (physical beauty, inner beauty, deformity and prejudice); *The Remains of the Day* (love, emotional repression); *My Boy Jack* (war, love, guilt); *The Naked Civil Servant* (gender, homosexuality, social attitudes). The rationale behind the use of movies in the classroom might easily end here.

But it need not. The use of movies can be given an even more, as it were, *structured* rationale in the teaching/learning process, particularly in *the practice and integration* of the four basic skills: reading, listening, speaking and writing.

It may be worth spelling this out, not least in view of the fact that progress in the language skills and their integration must owe much to *motivation*, and, if my own experience is anything to go by, people who are uninterested in cinema are like the proverbial hen's teeth. Teachers routinely encourage their students to watch movies in English – as though they needed much encouragement! A movie is a serious medium of communication, of entertainment, yes – but also of instruction. The four skills might be catered for thus:

Reading

Much here must depend on the kind of movie in question. The showing of a movie with a strong biographical element (a 'biopic'), like *The Elephant Man*, can be preceded by readings on the life of John (or Joseph) Merrick, on the Industrial Revolution, on the medical knowledge and competence of the times, on modern instances of the disease from which Merrick suffered, on different kinds of beauty. Or else, reading material is usually easy to find on the making, production and direction of the movie; there are some reviews, discussions of acting techniques and special effects, commentaries on the socio-economic conditions of the time and place in which the movie is set, and so on. Since the writing of student reviews may well feature later, it would be desirable to give examples of how reviews may be written, even before the movie is watched, though not necessarily reviews of the same movie; students can be given a *feeling* for the kind of stuff that reviews are expected to contain with this kind of preliminary reading; and some reviews may even be literary masterpieces, containing insight and wit, and therefore be more suitable for more advanced students (e.g. Quentin Crisp's review of *Ernesto*, reprinted in *The Stately Homo*, ed. Paul Bailey, Bantam Press, 2000).

Listening

Apart from listening to the movie itself, interviews with actors and directors are abundant on YouTube and are an excellent source of listening practice; they often contain very valuable insights and are therefore not only good practice but edifying, too (e.g. the Michael Parkinson-Rowan Atkinson interview).

But what about listening *and* watching? Feelings are mixed about giving students a worksheet of questions to answer while the movie is running. However, I have found it best to provide key questions in advance, 'key' in the sense that they refer to important moments, lines, scenes, for which the questions can function as cues and clues. My own approach is to run through the questions before showing the movie, but not require that they are answered during the movie.

Speaking

After the movie, students can be grouped together to help each other answer the questions as best they can. Question-types are best mixed, some dealing with important points of detail (e.g. lexis, idiom, grammar structures) and some dealing with general 'gist' understanding, involving interpretation of meaning and the students' own feelings and reactions towards this or that line or scene or character, not forgetting questions about setting in time and space, about 'message(s)', about theme(s), and, of course, whether or not they enjoyed the movie and would recommend it to their friends; liking or disliking the movie must be supported with reasons. Finally, they feed back to the teacher, and this stage provides opportunities for checks on understanding and interpretation. In the questions asked, the teacher is functioning as facilitator and guide to future discussion and criticism. The questions are therefore supportive, functioning as a series of prompts and talking-points around which later discussion can rotate.

But suppose we dispose with all prior prompts and questions and leave students to their own and each other's devices, with only the movie itself and their own unaided impressions? Well, of course, this is possible, too. Either way, the movie generates discussion and therefore speaking practice, and this is what the teacher aims at. But the teacher's questions are devised to introduce important lexis into subsequent discussion, so that some structured or targeted practice of key lexis is ensured (we should also remember that some formal examinations require students to write a film or book or play review amongst the writing options provided).

Questions on the movie, whether given prior to a showing or presented later, whether they are devised by the teacher or whether they flow naturally from students themselves, can rarely be satisfactorily covered immediately after the showing, simply because of the constraints of time. No matter; they can form the parameters of discussion at the first available opportunity. The most interesting questions are really no more than *catalysts* of discussion. Students, paired or grouped, discuss the film's themes and messages, merits, demerits, key moments, scenes, lines, symbolism – all with the teacher hovering in unintrusive proximity, taking note of important gaps in lexis or mistakes of grammar structure that he can later address during the feedback session.

Writing

The obvious task here is to produce a review. By now ideas should be plentiful. Our task as teachers is to point out that the use of past tense verb structures are not appropriate (or certainly not straightforwardly appropriate) to the narration of plots in movie, book or play mode. Instead, we use predominantly the *present simple* verb tense or form.

But a review is actually a complex piece of writing, involving not simply the telling of the plot, but the expression of opinion and the explication and justification of opinion. The *language of opinion and justification* is therefore vital. In this kind of writing task there is a multiplicity of writing *functions*. A review is a mixed bag and not to be taken lightly, which is why the provision of examples of reviews across a small spectrum of movies was not such a bad idea in the preliminary **Reading** stage. The basic concepts and lexis of reviews – direction, casting, setting, plot, theme, message, pace, credibility, quality of acting, soundtrack, special effects, all need an airing.

Films are therefore a useful source of motivation in the practice and integration of the basic language skills, and is not simply a means of 'getting away from it all'. Or, better, though perhaps paradoxically, they are a means of doing both: of 'getting away from it all' and at the same time practising the four language skills. And the key to an understanding of the paradox is that a movie can 'take us out of ourselves' and into another and fascinating world, a world in which we can glimpse something other than such stuff as grammar structures and phrasal verbs, albeit one in which such things as grammar structures and phrasal verbs play a vital part; but in this other world, a pretend-real world, the elements of language are perhaps more obviously a means to an end rather than ends in themselves. Our fascination is with this world, not with the elements of language, however vital these elements may be.

Self-Development

Due to the nature of the medium itself, movies are likely to give us more direct, poignant, insights into a host of issues having to do with the socio-economic world, with personal relationships and conflicts of all kinds, than, say, a novel or an anecdote. This is why they help to exemplify and develop classroom topics and themes. Talking about what it might be like to look like John Merrick is likely to benefit enormously from having watched *The Elephant Man*, for example, and the film itself becomes a talking point and an aid to discussion of the themes involved in it. Talking about the relative importance of personal or family relationships as distinct from material or commercial success is likely to be much easier and, incidentally, much more fun, if everybody has watched *The Great Outdoors*, with John Candy being chased by a bald-headed grizzly bear. Some movies are also landmarks in our life experience; they can actually help to make a difference to the way in which we see each other, the way in which we see the world and the parts we play in it. Making such a difference is the stuff and substance of self-development, or at least the profounder versions of it.

Not to mention the socially cohesive function of *sharing the experience* of seeing John Candy chased by a bear, or of sharing the more moving scenes in *The Elephant Man*, while subsequent discussions with others about that shared experience can even on occasion serve to deepen the experience itself and perhaps also improve our understanding of the people we are sharing that experience with – or it might challenge assumptions, or prompt questions where there were none hitherto: might I not find myself wondering why it is that the person I am talking to was not affected or moved in the way I was, or to the extent I was, or perhaps not moved or affected at all, or why his attention or interest was completely elsewhere, somewhere that was of no interest to me whatsoever? Has he missed something? – or have I?

12

Political Correctness *versus* Common Sense[24]

Language is a phenomenon greater than the sum of its parts, and this becomes clear whenever we feel moved to express our opinions as to what the role of the teacher is or should be. Such opinions are, of course, expressions of what we believe education to be all about. There are tensions here. Those of us who believe, with the psychologist Alfred Adler, that education should somehow be about changing society 'for the better', will want to see teachers as instruments of social change, and will be frustrated with teacher-training courses which perceive the teaching of English as a matter of teaching 'parts', recognising little or nothing beyond the *sum* of parts. Such courses will focus on how best to teach grammar structures, phrasal verbs, and so on. Little attention will be paid to what language is all about, to what lies beyond the summation of its parts.

Adler believed that schools should be 'the prolonged arm of the family', but his discussion is couched in normative terms, what *should* be the case as distinct from what *is* the case, because he knew all too well that teachers are trained to go no further than the summation of parts, which is why, he would say, education, as it stands, can truly claim to do no more

24   *Modern English Teacher*, Vol 19, No 3, 2010

than preserve the *status quo*, and it was precisely the *status quo* that gave him sleepless nights; perhaps it should worry us, too. At the zenith of his writing Germany had already donned the Nazi yoke; far from having maintained the *status quo* Germany was in rapid moral decline, and soon the disease of Nazism would spread its tentacles much further afield; education was designed to serve the Nazi ethos, and thus became a tool of repression and a perversion of genuine inquiry. Education in the 'narrow' sense still continued, producing Nazi nuclear physicists who were eagerly taken under the wing of the USA at the close of the war. The continuing debate as to whether this was a morally defensible thing for the American administration to have done suggests that education has a broader sense than the mere accumulation and ingestion of facts and the ensuing achievement of academic laurels.

This is as good a place as any to make reference to an article entitled 'Teaching Global Issues'[25], which raises issues that are in dire need of a little airing in the current global political climate. Altan begins by stating the obvious, which is often a most salutary way to start. Our world is beset with many problems of fundamental importance: terrorism, ethnic conflicts, the proliferation of nuclear weapons, social inequality, culture loss... and the list goes on. He then discusses how we, as teachers, as educators, can help our students to be more aware of all this, and how teachers can help intercultural communication and understanding.

What is most interesting, not to say somewhat disquieting and confusing for some of his readers, is that he is reasserting the role of teachers as instruments of social change. Personally, I have no quarrel with this, in principle. On the contrary, for many years now I have done my utmost to

---

25   Altan, *MET*, Vol 19, No 1

stress to my students that the learning of English, or of any language at all, is a key to infinite possibilities above and beyond the passing of examinations and the acquisition of academic and professional qualifications. The word 'key' hardly does the job! After all, without language, feelings, opinions, ideas, mindsets, ways of thinking and consequent action or inaction would all hang in a state of permanent suspension, if they existed at all.

The very idea that teachers of English as a foreign language should be 'instruments of social change' is anathema to those who believe that teachers should do no more than they are paid to do, which is to teach the elements, the parts, the bits, or, to use a relatively new piece of jargon, the 'chunks' of discourse, and nothing else. It has been for the most part an unwritten law that teachers should avoid topics like politics and religion in the classroom if there should be any risk of offending this or that student. ('Don't bring politics into the classroom,' teachers were once told by a director of studies who had clearly forgotten that it was already there and had never left.) But if this law is sufficiently generally and strictly applied, the teaching that is consequent upon it is what we might call *counterfeit teaching*. Why is it counterfeit? Because teaching English, teaching *language*, is not like teaching someone how to drive a car. To learn to drive you must practise driving, but you do not need to discuss global issues in the process; indeed, it is better for your concentration, and therefore for your driving, if you discuss nothing at all. But the practice of meaningful discussion is part and parcel of what it means to make meaningful progress in language acquisition. And it will not do to make a series of bland and simple statements, not even at the level of the Cambridge First certificate, let alone beyond.

Quite simply, the practice of the language, the exercise and development of all the principal language skills, requires the ability to discuss matters of global importance of the kind listed by Altan; it simply cannot be helped, and we should all be the poorer if it could. And yet, if we have German students in our classes, teachers may well feel obliged to follow the less than golden unwritten rule: 'Don't mention the war!' And with such an injunction, as though with a single stroke of the pen, the whole war is written off as a one-off point of historical reference, let alone a topic of discussion and debate. It is almost as though this mindblowing slice of history never really happened at all. (Rather Orwellian, is it not?) Perhaps the rule is unwritten precisely because it is so obnoxious, as though it is ashamed to show itself in public. In terms of the rule, a teacher might well feel precluded from providing thought-provoking instances of type 3 conditionals:'If Hitler had not invaded Russia, he might have won the war in Europe'; and even more irresistible 'mixed' conditionals like 'If Hitler had won the war, the world would be a very different place now and we would most probably not be sitting here right now learning about mixed conditional sentences!' After all, both historical speculation and personal speculation are expressible in sentences of this type.

None of this is intended as brief against sensitivity in the classroom. It is certainly not a question of causing offence gratuitously. It is not right to open old wounds merely for the macabre pleasure of seeing what is inside. It is not a question of apportioning blame to the students under one's charge or of delivering broadsides of reproach. The classroom is not the hustings and should not become a political platform. (We might suggest *en passant* that if freedom of speech should never be exercised when there is even the remotest possibility that someone somewhere might be offended, then it is hardly worth the candle, let alone worth fighting for! And our hallowed premise that democracy should be preserved is back to front and upside down.) Of course, sensitivity is a cardinal virtue; it might be cruel to enter knowingly upon a very sore point. Who in their right minds would want to address the subject of the rights and wrongs of abortion knowing full well that the tearful student in the back row has just had one, on pain of being disowned by her 'loving' parents if she had refused to go through with it? Who would invite a provocative debate on the pointlessness of religion knowing that the poor fellow at the back of the room has just recently suffered a bereavement and that he is now being comforted by the Italian priest sitting beside him? (Foreign priests do occasionally attend classes to learn English!) These are matters of delicacy, sensitivity and plain courtesy.

The flip side, however, is that a runner who constantly looks over his shoulder is unlikely to win the race and perhaps will never cross the winning line at all. Likewise, a writer who constantly worries about how his thoughts will be taken may demonstrate a good heart but can hardly give of his best; a speechmaker who constantly stumbles over his words will lose his audience together with his train of thought. That said, sensitivity is an unquestionable virtue.

Sadly, however, what is unquestionable is often employed as a prop for something else which is decidedly questionable. For the injunction that one should not cause offence gratuitously is thought to sit comfortably with all that is allowed to pass muster under the heading 'political correctness'. Political correctness, however you wish to slice it, is perhaps the most cancerous and the most terminal of all 'intellectual' and social diseases, for it is anathema to critical thinking, to the disposition and ability to ask questions, to the desire to follow them through once asked, to the notion, in a nutshell, of *following the logos* wherever it may lead. After all, Socrates paid the ultimate price for questioning the political correctness of his day, as did Jesus Christ and the Nazi dissidents, who came after him. We may say of people like this what Winston Churchill said in reference to the British fighter pilots in the Battle of Britain: Never in the history of intellectual and moral dissension has so much been owed by so many to so few. At best, political correctness run riot is the fanaticism of counter-fanaticism, and therefore abhorrent as itself a species of fanaticism.

Teachers of English as a foreign language, insofar as they are a species of educator *distinct from all others*, may be thought by some to be beyond or above or below all this. When I began my career in TEFL such matters were never discussed, not because they were not important then, but because political correctness had not yet established itself as a universal and unshakeable creed. And strongly extant, though never written or explicit, was the banal notion that language was no more than the sum of its parts and that it was the teacher's job merely to confine himself to addressing them, one by one.

Now we know, or should know, better, now that we have had the opportunity to breathe the fresh, invigorating oxygen of some degree of intellectual refinement. We know that language is necessary to all thinking, good or bad, to decency and to brainwashing. And we also know that we live in a world in which the chips are forever down. The chips are down, because, thanks to the killing power made possible by technological progress and nuclear fusion in conjunction with the very obvious failings of all that we encapsulate in the phrase 'human nature', we are faced with the choice of living together or dying together, of tolerating each other or despising each other. The way out of this Hobson's Choice is through greater understanding, and fundamental to this is better communication. Enter Language Greater than the Sum of its Parts!

Either you are a teacher who believes that your job is one whose value must extend outside the classroom, or you are one who tows the old party line that language is no more than the sum of its parts. No-one who has bothered to read my contributions to this publication will doubt where I myself stand. For many years now I have believed it essential to encourage students to think for themselves, to develop their critical faculties through the learning of English as a foreign language, to ask questions, to follow them through, as every good *parent* should do. Here we hit upon the essential difference between *what* to think and *how* to think. But political correctness is such a roughly hewn and uncultivated creature that it instinctively fails to distinguish the two. It consistently believes that encouraging people to think for themselves is tantamount to telling them what to think. *Logic, if anything,* should tell them *what* to think, and no-one, teachers included, invented logic. The ever-increasing conflation of 'how' and 'what' is a classic case of self-projection. Political correctness sees itself in a mirror and judges all alike. Not that fear has nothing to do with it – fear of rocking the boat. Altan suggests that global issues should find a place in lesson-plans by providing a focus each week on a different world problem. But amongst the examples he very properly cites are precisely those which political correctness would have us most wary of tackling: international terrorism, human rights, racism.

The sham and the shame of political correctness are aided and abetted by what purport to be strands of enlightened thinking. One such strand is cited favourably by Altan himself, which he calls 'cultural relativism'[26]

---

26   Readers interested in more esoteric discussions of some aspects of philosophical relativism (as distinct from so-called 'cultural relativism') may find it in my articles, 'Was Collingwood a Relativist?' in *Collingwood Studies* Vol V 1998, published by the R.G. Collingwood Society, and 'Some Forms of Relativism: An Analogical Model', *International Studies in Philosophy*, xxx111/4, 2001)

which he opposes to the foul brute 'ethnocentrism', this latter being a species of cultural insularity which judges inferior any culture other than one's own, a kind of cultural snobbishness. However, as a result of increased 'intercultural competence', says Altan, students will come to judge another culture by its context, and this is called 'cultural relativism'. My quarrel with this is that 'cultural relativism' does not imply 'moral relativism', and yet these two vastly different things are frequently and popularly conflated. When considering the erstwhile practice, amongst the Cheyenne Indians of the Northern Plains, to skin their captives alive, or of their brethren the Lakota Sioux to burn the hides off enemies who surrendered without putting up a fight, a cool consideration of historical and cultural contexts is no doubt a welcome aid to an increased understanding of such barbarism. But as the normative word 'barbarism' suggests, my understanding of such contexts in no way implies my moral acceptance of these practices; indeed, my abhorrence of them is in no way diminished. Understanding why something is done does not imply that it should be done. It is for this reason that the expression 'cultural relativism' is an unhappy one, since it may suggest to us that, having understood the context, our moral acceptance of that practice can be expected to follow as a matter of course. The fact is that such a species of cultural relativism ranks with political correctness as one of the cardinal intellectual diseases of our times, each lending to the other a *prima facie* credibility. In a world where 'anything goes', we shall find that nothing goes.

This is not to say that Altan is himself a moral relativist. On the contrary, for having specified Gardner's list of 'intelligences', and having noted that Gardner could not find a place for 'moral intelligence' on the grounds that it is 'normative' as distinct from 'descriptive', he goes on to say that we really cannot ignore the possibility that there is such a thing, because such a thing as 'a universal moral code' is crucial to help us rid the world of its evils. After all, lack of moral intelligence is abundant, for cleverness does not imply goodness. Clever business people are often greedy and devious, clever academics are often vainglorious, clever leaders murder millions in the name of abhorrent political creeds, and abhorrent religions pull the wool over the eyes of multitudes, and specific examples in each category are endless – all of which reveals monumental stupidity *of a kind*.

It is of course notoriously difficult to argue the case for a universal moral code that is *truly* universal or truly universal on *all* points of one and the same compass. To draw up a code and expect universal acceptance is therefore a specious form of wishful thinking. Ghandi seemed to think that the only code worth talking about was a simple one, namely that enshrined in the Sermon on the Mount, and that neither Christianity nor any other form of religion has anything further to add on the matter. Perhaps at sufficient level of generality it may be possible to find a set of rules that everyone other than bigots and the insane can accept without too much fuss: the sanctity of human life, for example, and the consequent refusal to accept the doctrine of an eye for an eye, a tooth for a tooth; kindness; compassion; understanding; tolerance, and, above all, love, which in any case seems to encapsulate all the rest. But, then, bigotry and madness are never in short supply, and mindless acts of terrorism would throw the principle of the sanctity of human life right back in our faces, which is why we call them mindless. And as for the Sermon on the Mount, Sir Thomas More is thought to have remarked that the English aristocracy would have snored right through it. But not only the English aristocracy, I would hasten to add.

Much as I should love to pursue the matter to the extent it truly deserves, this is not really the place to do so. I would only say that the distinction between the normative and the descriptive that Gardner and others take so much for granted is a irritating variant on the ancient theme that fact cannot imply value and value cannot imply fact, or that *ought* cannot imply *is* and *is* cannot imply *ought*, and this distinction is equally questionable on the grounds that a statement of 'bare fact' hardly exists. 'The old lady was killed in the explosion' is as much a statement of fact as one could strain to give, yet the statement invites us to *regret* the fact expressed and even to *condemn* the factors that led to her death even before we know what they were. The language we use in what appears to be statements of bald fact already, as it were, contain the prescriptions we use to condemn the fact expressed. The fact-value debate is fundamentally flawed but continues to sting, like a stunned wasp. That said, like other great philosophical debates it contains much of interest and much that is true, but this is not the place to seek to do justice to it.

'Critical thinking,' says Altan, 'should be at the core of our educational ideals'. True, this is not an original idea, but it is certainly worth restating. The point is nicely articulated by John Locke in *Thoughts Concerning Education*, published in 1714: 'The object of study is an increase in the powers and activity of the mind, not an enlargement of its possessions'. (I sometimes offer this statement to more advanced students when discussing the topic of education and ask them to rephrase it.) However, Altan is certainly giving us a valuable and timely reminder, given of course that we TEFL teachers should see ourselves as educators and allow ourselves some ideals; granted also that we see English like any other language, as a phenomenon far greater than the sum of its parts; granted, too, that we refuse to see ourselves as mere purveyors of the crumbs that fall from the tables of 'real' teachers in other, far 'nobler', parts of the educational spectrum. Of course, critical thinking is *not* the same as criticism, for the criticism of some attitudes or beliefs may be as prejudicial and bigoted as they are. Therefore, objectivity and balance should be given pride of place in any creditable instance of critical thinking, and maintaining objectivity and balance is often no mean feat.

Yet it is precisely this which is tested in questions of the form, 'Write a balanced account of...', 'Produce balanced arguments for and against the statement that...', 'Examine the arguments for and against the view that...'. And these are the question types that are frequently to be met with in examinations like IELTS (International English Language Testing Service), for they test the critical skills which are prerequisites of any meaningful university course, or any university course worthy of the name. It is also relevant to note here that examiners sometimes find fault with candidates who seem to think that the use of discursive-style sentence linking devices like 'On the one hand...', 'Furthermore,' 'Despite the fact that...' and so on, are sufficient to obtain a good pass, as though the provision of relevant supporting arguments and the adequate consideration of counterarguments was quite incidental, optional and inessential. In other words, it is as though candidates haven't the foggiest about what the phrase 'balanced argument' *means* – in which case they are hardly suitable candidates for such an examination and not yet ready to follow a university course. Understanding what 'balanced argument' means is, one would like to think, not only essential for a meaningful university experience, but also for any meaningful life; it is apt to recall the Socratic prescription that an unexamined life is not worth living, and J.S.

Mill's rejoinder to the objection that Socrates thought too much, namely that it is better to be a Socrates dissatisfied than pig satisfied.

Students wishing to enter British universities are required to employ the basic skills of critical thinking, and if they have not been taught these rudiments in their native countries, they are obliged to learn them now on pain of failing to enter, one continues to hope, a university in the UK. This may seem to many teachers a very tall order, if not a forlorn hope and a lost cause. Be that as it may, many university hopefuls seem to do well enough to have their aspirations more than amply met, such are the wonders of life. Wonders they certainly are, when we remember that critical thinking, as distinct from mere criticism, not only fails to be taught very well anywhere at all, but is in some countries positively discouraged if not strictly forbidden. Wittgenstein, in one of his notable analogies, once compared thinking with the attempt to keep a large rubber ball under the surface of the water with the palm of one's hand. Pressure forces it to the surface, and it's much easier just to give up and let the ball bounce to the surface and stay there rather than constantly applying pressure to keep it submerged. He was of course talking about *philosophical* thinking, and not the kind we routinely engage upon when, for example, deciding the relative merits of going out for a meal or staying at home and making a sandwich instead. Nevertheless, his analogy has some degree of application right across the board.

Critical thinking is not easy when we are required to do adequate justice to argument and counterargument, partly because it requires the exercise of the imagination. Moreover, 'following the logos wherever it may lead' is not something we are all capable of doing or of doing to the same extent, not forgetting, also, that it might lead to conclusions that we shall find surprisingly unwelcome or downright unsavoury. Courage, therefore, often has a place in the desire to allow logic and the facts full rein; logic and the facts, as distinct from what we have been subjected to by upbringing, tradition , conventional wisdom, the edicts of self-styled or dubiously appointed 'experts' and the unceasing, relentless, mindless propaganda of the mass media. Just think how many there are who are quite happy to condemn a book without having read it, or an opinion without even having understood it – just as many as there are who would embrace a set of ideas or a text, however obnoxious, simply on the hearsay of the foolish and the ignorant. In view of his dubious following, Karl Marx once declared that he was 'not a reliable Marxist', while Wittgenstein was constantly aware of the tendency to attract false disciples to an approach to philosophy they barely understood. The absence of independent thinking and the slavish attraction to cant, hypocrisy, mere propaganda and the mentality of the mob are unfortunate facts of life.

Lest it be thought that this contributor suffers from more than his fair share of 'ethnocentrism', I must say at once that I am often tempted to welcome my students on the first day of their courses to 'pre-Renaissance Britain'. If I am lucky, they will ask me what I mean. They do not ask me, for they have other things on their minds. No matter, for the rest of the course is dedicated to getting them to understand and employ, through the use of the language they are learning, the rudiments of critical thinking, those rudiments which were the preconditions of the Renaissance, and to apply them to everything, from the bits of grammar and lexis they are learning on a daily basis, to the consideration of global issues of the kind Altan refers to; for when they consider global issues they are employing the bits and pieces of language in order to go beyond them, as the steps of a ladder helps us to get elsewhere – somewhere different from where we started.

It used to be said that language is a key, which was meant not a key to money, gain or personal advancement, but to literature, to ideas, to understanding, to meaningful communication, and so to a better world. I don't hear this kind of thing very much now. Times have changed. So much for moving with them! For perhaps times have changed too much and in the wrong direction, which explains my temptation to talk in terms of pre-Renaissance Britain. It is perhaps a cynical phrase, but the country is now so much awash with political correctness, a neurotic hyper-sensitivity about doing, saying and thinking the 'right thing', that one often feels like giving up doing, saying and thinking altogether. (I am reminded about Wittgenstein's remark about wanting to utter an inarticulate sound.) Political correctness in the form it now threatens to develop into is not simply an inconvenience. It is anathema to the most fundamental tenets of critical thinking and is therefore the very last thing we want to see in a world beset with so equally fundamental problems. It points the way backward, not the way forward.

In one of his rare television interviews, Bertrand Russell, then fast approaching the end of his long life, was asked what advice he would wish to give to future generations. He limited himself to two short prescriptions, one intellectual, the other moral. In the former, he urged that we should always seek to be impartial and objective in the consideration of the facts; this was a prescription against prejudice of all kinds. His moral advice was encapsulated in the phrase 'hatred is foolish, love is wise'. He elaborated by saying that the world is interconnected and interdependent and that we cannot afford to be intolerant of one another; 'if we are to live together and not die together, we must learn a kind of charity', a level of tolerance that would help to mitigate the kind of hatred and bitterness which, if now unleashed, might end human civilisation for good. I often use this interview as a meaningful listening exercise in the classroom; it serves to show students what Cambridge was like in Russell's time, and how, difficult enough though the situation was then, the country has deteriorated even further now that political correctness has set in and spread its tentacles far field; for there is no-one like Russell now, and it is questionable whether his probing would be considered immune to political correctness; his pipe-smoking would also raise some eyebrows and even get him into trouble with the law. Russell's advice to future generations is simple, far too simplistic some would say, and it is infinitely easier to give than to follow; on this students are usually agreed; but the value of his sentiments is never lost on them, and, despite their diversities, sometimes very marked, they applaud the advice he gives. It is in their applause that we might yet see some glimmer of hope for the future; perhaps their English will be used to good effect in making so-called 'common sense' a lot more common than it is now.

It is perhaps in Russell's sentiments that we have the basis of some kind of 'universal moral code' of the sort to which Altan alludes. If so, it is still one we must *strive for*; for it cannot come all by itself. The value of Altan's article surely lies in this, that we are prompted to remind ourselves that as teachers of EFL we are still educators, that educators hemmed in by political correctness can hardly discharge their responsibilities as facilitators of independent and critical thinking, and that if this function is denied them, then education itself, though a house of many mansions, is not a house worthy of inhabitation. The most basic and enduring questions of all must surely be: What are we as teachers of EFL, and what are we really doing when we do it? I have always thought that we should enter the classroom leaving our personal or domestic problems behind. The same cannot be said of our humanity or of our responsibilities as thinking human beings, and here perhaps we have the beginnings of some answers to the questions here posed.

13

Language Patterns[27]

Knitting patterns are, or so I am told, easy to follow once you get going. It's just a question of getting the hang of them. That's the beauty of a pattern, *any* pattern: it's repeatable. And what is repeatable can be practised, and practice makes perfect. Herein also lies the beauty of patterns, whenever they are discoverable, in the business of teaching and learning a language. In this discussion I shall limit myself to two types of pattern. These patterns are useful in the teaching and practice of what we have come to call *discursive* English, the language of discussion or argument, both written and spoken.

Pattern 1

Most teachers who prepare candidates for examinations such as the International English Language Testing Service (IELTS), and the Cambridge Advanced (CAE) and Proficiency (CPE) examinations will agree that it is difficult to get their students to follow the rules of correct lexical and grammatical structure in the context of discussions of global topics like poverty, homelessness, education, terrorism, environmental pollution, and so on.

---

27   *Teaching English Professional*, Issue 75, July 2011

Topic names like these are abstract general uncountable nouns, and examination questions on such topics are not, of course, a test of the candidates' philosophical or political originality, but of their ability to, amongst other things, use such nouns according to the canons of correct English. These topic nouns are key words, so errors concerning them are properly regarded as fundamental. Moreover, the ability to use them correctly is often immediately apparent, because they so often feature in the first sentence, as when a candidate begins a talk or essay on the importance of education with 'The education is very important, because....'. Candidates who begin like this have, from the word go, demonstrated their inability to use the key word properly, eliciting sighs of despair and knitted brows from their examiners. Their very first word is an error!

The circumstances in which the definite article can be used with nouns like these need to be spelt out, for it is no easy matter. A candidate's L1 may well contain articles, but the rules of usage may be different (as in French, Italian and Spanish); or they may contain articles of an entirely different species, if we recognise them as articles at all (as in Chinese, Japanese, Korean and Turkish).

So what? Well, simply this: a pattern is something that can be *followed*. And then, once you get the hang of it, well... Consider the following text:

'Unemployment is a very serious issue. The unemployment of the younger generation, in particular, is a problem that should concern us all. The unemployment of very large numbers of people obviously affects the social and economic fabric of society as a whole, and this could have disastrous effects on the political future of the country concerned. There are many other issues that should worry us.

However, unemployment is not something that can be ignored indefinitely, because the unemployment of the 1920s and 30s in Western Europe taught us lessons we should never forget.'

Can we make out a pattern here? Well, who are you asking? If my native language is one which doesn't use articles in the same way, and one which uses articles in ways in which I myself am not at all clear about, the pattern may yet be lost on me. So, let's try again, and this time with a topic which may touch us all even more closely than unemployment:

'Love is a house of many mansions, which is to say that it is of many different kinds. The love of a person for his job is very different from the love between mother or father and child. The love of a man or woman for their partner is very different from the love of music or of art. The love for one's job is different from the love of the composer for his music. The love of mathematics is not the same as the love between Romeo and Juliet. The philosopher Bertrand Russell says that love is wise and hatred is foolish. What kind of love is he talking about?'

Is the pattern clear now? No? Well, let's try again. This time the topic is poverty:

'Poverty is a global issue. The poverty of so-called third-world countries has been much publicised. However, the poverty we can associate with, for example, the poorest quarters of Brasilia, is abject and totally unacceptable. Although poverty is on the political agenda of most civilised countries, the poverty we only occasionally hear about is almost beyond belief. Discussions of poverty should therefore take into account the poverty which most civilised people would consider totally reprehensible in modern times.'

Still not clear? No matter, we could go on and on, through pollution, hunger, inflation, drug addiction, beauty... Let's try beauty:

'Beauty is of different kinds. The beauty of mathematics is very different from the beauty of Mother Theresa or Jesus Christ. The beauty we may associate with a piece of music is very different from the beauty of Catherine Zeta Jones. The beauty of Catherine Zeta Jones is not the beauty Don McLean sings about in the song "Starry, Starry Night". Beauty is not, therefore, one thing. It is not easy to talk about beauty without talking about the beauty of very different things.'

Abstract general nouns take the definite article in such constructions as '*the* + noun + *of*,' '*the* + noun + *between*', and so on, which are constructions of greater *specificity*. They also require the definite article in clauses which take *which* or *that*, or in clauses where *which* or *that* can be employed but are omitted according to the preference of the writer or speaker.

The point here, however, is not to argue the grammar of general abstract nouns, but merely to point out the importance of establishing patterns which students should then be encouraged to imitate. We can also present students with the *wrong* pattern and invite them to correct it:

'The beauty is a house of many mansions, which means that it is of different kinds. Beauty of mathematics is very different from beauty of Mother Teresa or Jesus Christ. Beauty we may associate with a piece of music is very different from beauty of Catherine Zeta Jones. Beauty of Catherine Zeta Jones is not beauty Don McLean sings about in "Starry, Starry Night". The beauty is not, therefore, one thing. It is not easy to talk about the beauty without talking about beauty of very different things.'

Texts demonstrating correct or incorrect patterns can be presented in a variety of ways, including short passages for *dictation* by the teacher or by students themselves. The aim is to teach our students to knit the language together by following the correct patterns.

Having established the pattern and exemplified it in written English, it might now be time to try it out in spoken English. Aspects of the pattern may be made more memorable by inviting students to discuss, for example, Plato's idea that 'The purpose of education is to teach us to love beauty'[28], or how about Dostoyevsky's 'The world will be saved by beauty'[29]? Note: *The* world, not *world*; and *beauty*, not *the* beauty.) Less ambitiously (!) we might ask them to discuss the importance of education, not of *the* education, and, hopefully, they will talk about *the* education of children and *the* education of adults, and not education of children and education of adults.

Pattern 2

My second structural pattern which I believe students should be encouraged to imitate also shows us the practical, sociological function of grammar, and

---

28   *The Republic*, Part 3, Bk 3
29   *The Idiot*

because it relates grammar to real life and real life choices, it should appeal to students who very naturally seek a practical framework for the understanding of English grammar. Our general context is still discursive English. Again, consider topics such as pollution, violence, homelessness, poverty etc. The point is that we are providing students with a grammar 'framework' suitable for the discussion of many such topics; a framework is like a picture-frame: the picture may be changed, but the frame remains the same.

Type 1 conditional Sentence:

If we fail to address the problem properly, the consequences may be dire.

The consequences may be dire if we fail to address the problem properly.

If we should fail to address the problem properly, the consequences may be dire.

The consequences may be dire if we should fail to address the problem properly.

Should we fail to address the problem properly, the consequences may be dire.

The consequences may be dire should we fail to address the problem properly.

Type 2 conditional sentence:

If we failed to address the problem properly, the consequences could be dire.

The consequences could be dire if we failed to address the problem properly.

If we were to fail to address the problem properly, the consequences could be dire.

The consequences could be dire if we were to fail to address the problem properly.

Were we to fail to address the problem properly, the consequences could be dire.

The consequences could be dire were we to fail to address the problem properly.

Granted, teachers know best how to teach what they teach. But, once again, we have patterns, and patterns are repeatable. Consider the political/ sociological/psychological difference between 'If we fail to address the problem properly, the consequences may be dire', and 'Were we to fail to address the problem properly, the consequences may be dire'.

If you were a party leader contemplating the imminent elections and you had been preaching the importance of maintaining a positive attitude about your chances, you would much rather hear 'Were we to lose the election…' than 'If we lose the election…'.

Not very clear? Well, what about simple courtesy and sensitivity? Suppose a sensitive, hardworking but not exceptionally bright student is worried about his performance in next week's examination. Would you say 'If you fail, it won't be the end of the world', or 'Were you to fail, it wouldn't be the end of the world'? The decision is yours, but instinctively and in the interests of sensitivity, you might choose the latter as it doesn't express the possibility of failure quite as strongly as the former.

But the simple point here, as always, is that there are *patterns to practise*, and in the above examples I would argue that the differences between the choices are ones involving diplomacy and sensitivity; they are not simply straight alternatives differing purely in their structures.

The conditional forms given here are items which can be practised and applied to the topics denoted by abstract general nouns of the type we began by discussing. Sentences of this type are expected in discursive English, and the patterns and range of choices should be presented to students so that they can then apply them as appropriate. If we can get across to them such notions as sensitivity, diplomacy and common human decency, so much the better. After all, grammar should have evolved to suit our needs and our values, not vice versa.

Structural patterns are also found in retrospective judgements, judgements which should appeal to students for the same reasons they appeal to us all. Consider historical speculation:

If Charles I had defeated Cromwell, the course of English parliamentary history might well have been very different.

The course of English parliamentary history might have been very different had Charles I defeated Cromwell.

Had Charles I defeated Cromwell, the course of English parliamentary history might well have been very different.

The course of English parliamentary history might well have been very different if Charles I had defeated Cromwell.

Here, in c), we have a third-conditional pattern including *inversion*. And there are *mixed* third-conditionals in a) below:

If Charles I had defeated Cromwell, the present role of the British monarchy might be very different.

The present role of the British monarchy might be very different if

Charles I had defeated Cromwell.

Had Charles I defeated Cromwell, the present role of the British
monarchy might be very different.

The present role of the British monarchy might be very different had
Charles I defeated Cromwell.

And for more immediate effect, let's apply this to a student:

If Laura had stayed in Italy, she would have worked in a beauty salon.

Laura would have worked in a beauty salon had she stayed in Italy.

And so on…

The pattern continues. And the object is precisely to get students to go on
in the same way. Isn't that what we always try to do? We should try to help
students to think for themselves; their ideas, their opinions are matters of
their own choosing. However, whether or not they can *express* their ideas
and their views *correctly* in English is not a matter of their own choosing,
nor is it of ours as teachers. It is a question of the rules of correct usage.

* * *

Whether you are a student of mathematics or of a language, it is comforting
to be presented with the phrase 'and so on'. It means: 'If you've grasped the
point, you can go on by yourself with confidence.' If the point has not been
grasped, well at least we can try again. It may be true that 'the point' in
language is not what it is in mathematics. If it were, the Tower of Babel
would collapse in an instant. Even so, patterns can sometimes be found,

which is why we can speak of 'rules'. As teachers, our job is to understand patterns and point them out. 'Do it like *this*' means 'Do it as *we* do it', and doing it as we do it, when we do it *correctly*, means following a pattern.

14

Student Presentations: Technology in the Classroom[30]

Consider the following list of topics:

Rachmaninov

Sidney Poitier

Some Basic Elements of Aerodynamics

John Maynard Keynes

Winston Churchill

Philip II of Spain

Aspects of Racism

Plato on Love

Sexual Equality

Towards a Perfect World

New Zealand Explored

The Life of Sir Arthur Conan Doyle

These topics, I am delighted to say, were the subjects of student presentations over the last few months. All were carefully researched and also well received by the whole class, generating many interesting questions and some 'deep' and sometimes very lively discussions. Presentations are something I have been encouraging for years, but when I wrote about them last[31] I was thinking of them in terms of their role in the integration of skills and peer assessment. Hopefully, the whole point of presentations hardly needs to be laboured; they provide a focus for the integration of skills and subject context for class discussion. As I see it, presenters should be given as much time as they wish, both in the preparation stages and during the presentation itself; it is they who should choose the appropriate format for their presentations, guided, aided and abetted by the teacher, as necessary.

What of the role of technology, of the internet, of PowerPoint, of projectors and all the paraphernalia that are nowadays increasingly made available as a matter of course in the classroom?

The simple truth is that all the topics listed above could have been presented without aids of any kind at all, save perhaps a few bullet points written on a scrap of paper as an *aide memoire*. Had they been so presented, the focus would have been very squarely on the *presenter* and what the presenter had to say. And far from there being anything objectionable in this, the presentation would have achieved its central aim, which is to practise English as a medium of communication: the language of description, of explanation, of response to question and comment. All the elements of clear communication would have been put to the test, which is precisely the rationale behind the activity: the use of adjectives, syntax,

---

31   *MET*, Vol 14, No 2, 2005

lexical collocation, cohesive devices, to say nothing of pronunciation and clarity of enunciation.

I state the obvious. But I do so because the obvious is also important, and what is important is often forgotten or given less than its fair due. One very obvious truth is that very successful presentations just do not require the use of state-of-the-art technology. But we should go even further than this and add to this heresy yet another, by declaring that the use of state-of-the-art technology can actually *militate against* successful presentations. However, it is essential that I am not accused falsely, that I am not now accredited with the *wrong* kind of heresy.

Therefore, let it be stated without further ado that with only one or two exceptions (not perhaps too difficult to guess) all the topics in my list were presented with PowerPoint technology and the use of the internet. Further, let it be granted that 'in the modern world' (Heaven help us!) the use of state-of-the-art technology in the presentation of ideas is now, or is very fast becoming, a universal and unquestioned fact of life. So, in the appraisal of a presentation in terms of the extent to which *communication in and through the language* has been achieved, we must now add the element, not of the *use* of technology, but of the *judicious* use of technology.

The principle of the judicious use of presentation aids is of course simple, and it is applicable to the most basic (should we now say 'primitive'?) of aids: blackboards and, their successors, whiteboards. When the presenter writes on the whiteboard, is his handwriting legible? Does he stand back from the board to allow his audience to see what he has written? I am pained to recall a presentation in which the presenter blocked the view of his audience, and, when asked to stand aside so that what he had written could actually be seen, it turned out that his scribble was illegible! A double whammy! On another occasion, a map drawn on the whiteboard and purportedly of Brazil might just as well have been one of the Irish coastline. Such blunders are obvious deficiencies in basic presentation skills, and may even suggest deficiencies of another kind. Granted, some deficiencies in presentation skills can actually be obviated by the use of PowerPoint technology.

New technology presents us with new possibilities. However, as with all human developments, new possibilities are not inevitably new steps forward. Every new possibility is also a possibility for error, which is perhaps one reason why the philosopher Wittgenstein once remarked that it is in the nature of every advance that it should seem greater than it is, and why the Preacher lamented that there is nothing new under the sun. Be that as it may, when people wax lyrical on the theme 'exciting new possibilities', they are not, or hopefully not, excited by the possibility of error. And one significant error, particularly in the context of language teaching, is the belief that a good presentation is defined *solely* by whether the technology succeeds – as if to suggest that whether the presenter has practised the language of communication, or practised it sufficiently well and sufficiently correctly is quite secondary. Now who in his right mind would entertain such a belief? It might be better to ask: Who in his right mind would entertain such a belief knowingly and expressly? For it is quite astonishing how many such erroneous beliefs are held unknowingly and inexpressly, as though they are only half-believed.

Obvious falsehoods are just as important as obvious truths. Falsehoods point to danger. In language teaching, the danger of technological aids is of course that they may be allowed to *take over*, so that the presentation becomes less an opportunity to practise speaking skills, to put one's point over orally, to describe, explain, elucidate, argue, and more an opportunity *to show what technology can do* – as though the technology is being tested or put on show, and not the presenter's language skills! And what technology can do is not always what is intended, and is not always desirable. If, for example, it is allowed to rob a presenter of the opportunity to *present* by demonstrating the very language skills he is supposed to be learning and practising.

Equally obvious, however, is that the ability to point one's point across, to exercise oral skills and to use technology effectively are not mutually exclusive. In fact, there might even be a case for sometimes allowing the technology to take over, as when, in the event, the topic proves too much for the presenter and 'nerves' get in the way; in such a case the technology can allow him to save face; in such a case, the technology can allow the presenter to play at least a supporting role. But this is a default position, and clearly the presentation has not worked. Recently, a presenter, not the sort who is troubled by 'nerves', simply stood before the class, introduced the topic woodenly in three clipped sentences, clicked the mouse two or three times and invited us to watch a video on YouTube with the words 'YouTube can do it better than me'! Once again, the presentation hadn't worked, because it hadn't really taken place, despite the fact that the video was compelling viewing. However, even here the presenter can at least claim to have introduced the topic, and hopefully his self-esteem will have benefited to some small extent.

In general, we might say that a presenter is supported by technology in the way that a budding musician is supported by a good quality instrument, and we must remember that someone learning to play a musical instrument is, although not yet proficient, still producing *music* in the process of learning how to produce *better* music. But in the case of the presenter who resorted to a YouTube video for the whole session,

I am reminded of a school concert in which the violinist approached his position on the stage professionally, tuned his instrument professionally while the audience waited patiently for musical wonders to be performed, adopted a professional posture and adjusted the violin under his chin professionally... and then proceeded to produce the most disharmonious and disquieting screeching sounds known to man, reminiscent perhaps of a cat relentlessly chased by giant mice; what had promised to be a musical presentation turned out to be a monumental disaster.

Ideally, of course, we aim for equilibrium between the skilful use of technology and the practice of speaking skills to their optimum effect.

I would say that this balance was pretty nicely achieved for the presentation of the topics listed at the beginning of this discussion. Almost everyone used the internet, in particular YouTube, to illustrate what they had said or were about to say or to enunciate some general discussion: clips from speeches, films, documentaries, or simply still pictures. And although the use of such technology is not demanded by the topics in question, it is often expected these days and taken for granted, even in non-professional contexts – which just goes to show how deep and extensive a role is now played by what we call 'technological innovation'.

The essential point in all this is *the practice of the language*, not primarily a demonstration of the ability to flick switches and click buttons; clicking and flicking through a presentation is no indication of language skills. Agreed, a presentation can be enhanced by state-of-the-art technology, and this kind of enhancement is hardly possible unless we assume an ability to flick the right switches and click the right buttons, and all at the right time. But it is easy to be carried away by 'exciting new possibilities' to the extent that we forget where our priorities should lie. Nor should we be upset or disappointed if a presenter wishes to address the class with nothing more than a scrap of paper in his hands. Aping Wittgenstein, perhaps we might say that it is in the nature of human beings that they should tend to lose sight of their priorities when faced with every new advance. A car is a means of transport, we use it to get from A to B; everyone wishes for a pleasant journey, and a car enhances the trip; but our priority is to *arrive*, and hopefully in one piece.

If the essential point is the practice of the language, then essential to this is *motivation*. Technology can help foster motivation. If a presenter can *illustrate* his presentation with moving images in a kind of instant cinema, or if he can raise images and speeches and interviews to support his thesis or to explain his enthusiasm for the topic he presents, then so much the better. It is precisely *this* that constitutes an 'exciting possibility', not simply the screen dexterity that comes with, for example, an addiction to video games and 'surfing the net' or an obsession with Facebook. (Whenever I refer to a person, I try to show my students a picture of the person in question – so that they have a face to attach to the reference; for me, to do this online and at the drop of a hat is an 'exciting possibility' and enhances the reference I am making.)

Technology can help foster motivation. But what comes first is motivation arising from interest in the topic presented. It is interest in the topic that makes the technology an 'exciting possibility', not the technology that inspires interest in the topic. For example, if you are inspired by the achievements of Sidney Poitier, it is this that renders what you can do with the technology an 'exciting possibility', not the possibilities of technology that inspire your interest in Sidney Poitier. How wonderful to see and to hear the actor giving his moving acceptance-speech for a

Lifetime Achievement award – thanks to YouTube. Why? Clearly, because we are interested in the man and his achievements, not because we are moved by YouTube! A student may come to me excitedly with an idea for presentation. It is the subject that holds his interest; it is the subject that he wants to hold forth about; and just how he is going to go about it, important though this obviously is, comes second. Pretty evident, isn't it? It is simply for this reason that the use of state-of-the-art technology is neither a necessary nor a sufficient condition of a successful student presentation. It may be desirable; but it is not necessary; it may offer enhancement, but it is not by itself sufficient. Technology, especially computers and computer-dependent gadgetry, have a way of beguiling us all. We should beware the ghost in the machine!

15

Teacher Motivation[32]

Whenever 'culture' is deemed a dirty word, the light in the lighthouse of civilisation flickers and dims; it is not yet, one dares to hope, quite extinguished. Some phrases now have a wide and sloppy currency: 'pop culture', 'celebrity culture', 'youth culture', 'business culture', 'hi-tech culture', 'computer culture'. What on earth do they mean? The word 'culture' is like a hat worn by so many different heads that it has become quite shapeless. Are these 'cultures' really the antithesis of culture properly conceived? Are they distortions or perversions of culture rightly conceived? But what *is* culture 'properly, rightly, conceived'? It is depressingly suggestive that the question needs to be asked at all or that answer has to be reworked – suggesting perhaps that the light in the lighthouse of civilisation has dimmed so far that the wick is badly in need of trimming before we are left entirely in the dark and our ships founder on the rocks. What for that matter is 'civilisation'? We speak of ancient civilisations which practised human sacrifice; but then we say that human sacrifice is uncivilised. Clearly there is a normative element here: we *describe* an ancient civilisation; but we *judge* its practices as morally right or wrong. And perhaps when we speak of 'culture' while denouncing its pretenders, we are also making a normative assessment.

We must start somewhere. I shall start with the assertion that, fundamentally, culture, however we *use* the word, cannot be divorced from language; language and culture are inextricably linked. So, when we speak about culture 'rightly conceived' as distinct from its pretenders, we are making a normative judgement. And such judgements may have to do with *standards*; so that when we speak of 'language' we are not speaking of just *anything* that might count on some criterion as language, like the grunts and exclamations of excited gorillas or the outpourings of drunken yobs.

Getting our terms right is vital, because the subject we are now discussing has to do with the true value of learning and teaching a language, and is therefore bound up with our true value as teachers, and with questions as to what we *should* teach; should we for example teach the outpourings of drunken yobs, and, if so, what reason – as models to emulate or as examples to despise? It is bound up with the *integrity* that we give to our jobs, our *self-esteem* as teachers and the *respect* we should accord to our students.

But it is particularly teachers that concern me here. Much has been said, and much has been assumed, about the importance of motivating students. It is high time something was said about the motivation of teachers. Since it is useless to speak in terms of high pecuniary rewards, it seems to me that serious motivation must be sought elsewhere – for example, when teachers recognise the true value of their profession; but, as I see it, no-one underestimates the value of the work teachers do more than teachers themselves. Although they will without hesitation agree that their jobs have value, it seems to me that they have not even begun to appreciate just how and in what sense their work can be considered amongst the most valuable contributions anyone can make to human life, and, I dare to say it, 'civilisation rightly conceived'. If asked to explain the value of their work, they might glib appeals to the importance of something vaguely called 'communication', or they might say that their jobs have to do with helping students to study something else through the medium of English, or simply that it helps students to get jobs, or better jobs, and so on.

But none of this even remotely touches the real importance of what they are doing and, arguably, what they *should* be doing; what is often said in explanation of the importance of language teaching is evasive and quite besides the point, even though what they say is *perfectly true* – teachers do indeed help their students in the ways vaguely outlined, and this is not *un*important. Nevertheless, such explanations are thin, limp and unconvincing when it comes to the provision of teacher motivation; they beg more questions than they will ever be capable of answering. In fact, in giving such explanations, however innocuous they seem to be, teachers are in fact badly short-changing themselves. Such explanations seem to treat language merely and solely as a means to an end, as if to suggest that were there a cheaper, faster, less harrowing alternative, students might just as well take it, because it is only the 'end' that really counts. They fail to see that in a profound sense, the means and the end in language teaching are inextricably linked, and in this sense the connection between teaching and financial reward is irrelevant. The advice 'If it's money you're after, don't be a teacher' is perfectly reasonable; but it is precisely *because* it is valid that it is evidence that we teachers must be doing something extraordinarily valuable, for when in the history of our much vaunted 'civilisation' has the work teachers do been justly rewarded in any pecuniary sense? Little wonder, then, that Socrates and countless others like him received their 'just desserts' according to the perceptions of 'the powers that be', perceptions that have held sway for centuries, are frustratingly slow to change and promise to run their full course throughout the history of 'civilised' man on this poor planet.

To put some flesh on these bare bones and shed some welcome light on what I believe to be the true value of the work teachers do, I should like to take as my text one of the last essays of an unusually perceptive historian, Tony Judt, in an article entitled 'If words fall into disrepair, what will substitute? They are all we have'[33]. Suffering from a neurological disorder which was progressively depriving him of the power of speech, Judt was brought to realise more than ever before the importance of words, of language, and the article in question was something in the order of a final plea, one which we as teachers of language would do well to heed.

Judt states that as an undergraduate his faith in articulacy was strengthened, and it seemed that articulacy was not simply *evidence* of intelligence, but intelligence *itself*. He agrees that rhetorical facility is not to be equated with originality and depth of content, but, at the same time, inarticulacy does suggest a deficiency of thought.

This idea will sound odd to a generation praised for what they are trying to say rather than the thing said. Articulacy became an object of suspicion in the 1970s: the retreat from 'form' favoured uncritical approbation of 'mere self expression', above all in the classroom. But it is one thing to encourage students to express opinions freely, and to take care not to crush these under the weight of prematurely imposed authority It is quite another for teachers to retreat from formal criticism in the hope that the freedom thereby accorded favours independent thought: 'Don't worry

33   Tony Judt, *The Guardian*, 10 August 2010

how you say it, it's the ideas that count.'

However well-meaning this reaction against articulacy, it is inherently confused and is no aid to the expression of intelligent opinion. For *how* you say something is not an entirely different creature from *what* you say. (Not to be confused with the distinction between *what* you say and whether you are *sincere* about what you say.) This sloppy form of reaction is paralleled elsewhere: in the possibly well-meaning attempt to encourage perseverance; a few meaningless scribbles are called a 'work of art' when they are *not*; a few knocks on the table are described as 'a piece of music' when they only a few knocks on the table! To many people, it is obviously ridiculous to equate rubbish with art; but, to many others, distinctions between art and mere scribbling, or between music and plain noise, are either invalid or, at best, delightfully blurred. Alarm bells should certainly be ringing, for quite frequently the voice of outspoken but valid criticism is met with a barrage of hostility, as if to suggest that valid criticism is by definition *morally* objectionable. Alarm bells should be heard, because if we allow that *anything goes*, it must follow that *nothing* does. In a world where anything goes, we lost everything that matters, past, present and future.

If *how* we say something is not an entirely different creature from *what* we say, there are obvious implications for those of us engaged in TEFL and charged with the task of teaching *academic writing* in preparation for examinations which test the skill of formal discursive writing. For academic *writing* is not an entirely different creature from academic *thinking*. Teaching academic writing, if it is to be more than the parrot-production of a set of discursive linking devices and clichéd phrases ('I simply cannot subscribe to the view that...'; 'However...'; Therefore...'; 'In the final analysis…' etc.) means encouraging students to *think*, for *academic writing* is the expression of *academic thinking*. The ability to produce academic English is, if it is to be more than stylistically going through the motions, the ability to think academically. And 'going through the motions' is just an elongated synonym for 'pretence', which leaves intellect out of account altogether. (We are reminded of so-called 'celebrity culture' in which mere celebrity is confused with real talent or skill.) No wonder both examiners and teachers, or at least those with sufficient integrity, have complained that candidates simply trot out formal sentence-linking devices, often doing so inappropriately and inaccurately, without ever actually answering the question set, and in some cases without ever even *addressing* them – a frustration vented in the plea: 'Please answer the question!' In answer to those who object: 'Yes, but it isn't easy to exercise the intellect in a foreign language,' the response is surely: 'Well, it's a necessary part of the territory!' It's not easy for learner drivers to concentrate on where they are going while at the same time operating the controls, but…

Returning to our text, Judt writes: 'Forty years on from the 60s there are not many instructors left with the self-confidence (or training) to pounce on infelicitous expression and explain clearly why it inhibits intelligent reflection…' As distinct from centuries past when 'how you expressed a position corresponded closely to the credibility of your argument … Confused words suggested confused ideas at best, dissimulation at worst.' But surely technology has vastly improved communication? Alas, alack, another myth, as though we hadn't enough of those already. Judt goes on: 'Cultural insecurity begets its linguistic doppelgänger. The same is true of technical advance. In the world of Facebook, Myspace and Twitter (not to mention texting), pithy allusion substitutes for exposition. Where once the internet seemed an opportunity for unrestricted communication, the commercial bias of the medium – "I am what I buy" – brings impoverishment of its own. My children observe of their own generation that the communicative shorthand of their hardware has begun to seep in to communication itself: "People talk like texts." The disease does not stop there: 'Shoddy prose today bespeaks intellectual insecurity: we speak and write badly because we don't feel confident in what we think and are reluctant to assert it unambiguously ("It's only my opinion…"). Rather than suffering from the onset of "newspeak", we risk the rise of "nospeak". Communicating as distinct from texting is vital, because it is 'not just the means by which we live together but part of what living together means'.

I have quoted Judt at length, because the issues he raises are enormously far-reaching. Perhaps it is, amongst other things, the advent of what Judt calls 'nospeak' that encourages the impression that human beings have become *en masse* subject to a downward intellectual mutation, that the human race is a slave to its own technology such that morally and intellectually we are all in reverse gear, that we are on this downward course unsuspectingly – worse, that we imagine that we have never been cleverer and better than we are now!

Judt was not thinking specifically of TEFL when he wrote these things. No matter, he *might* have been. Meaningful communication, substance, articulacy, thought, in art, in music, in speaking and in writing – all this is what culture 'properly conceived' is, and this is why it is worth preserving and worth passing on, in just the way that civilisation is worth preserving and passing on, because the best our civilisation has to offer embodies, consists of, *is*, culture 'properly conceived'. If anything is done, it should be done to improve what we have, not diminish it. This is why students should be taught rules and standards and, with these, encouraged to acquire the ability, not merely the wherewithal by rote, to express ideas with accuracy, using words as the building bricks of sentences and sentences as reliable expressions of ideas. Perhaps an all too frequent refusal to acknowledge the importance of articulacy is why examiners sometimes complain of the paucity of answers to written questions, or say that candidates provide only the *form* of an answer without the *substance*, or that they speak in cliché without ever expressing an intelligent opinion. The ability to *answer the question* presupposes the ability to use the language correctly, and articulacy is not served by a woolly approach to the teaching of language; we should not apologise for the rules of the game, particularly when the game is well worth playing.

Nor should teachers apologise for what they do, or view what they do with only a modicum of grudging esteem, as though they feel, or are invited to feel, in some way weakened or devalued because what they do will not allow them to enjoy the lifestyles of merchant bankers and pop stars or the praise of kings. If they are precluded from enjoying the trappings of wealth and celebrity, it is perhaps an inability in the light of which they should take heart, for it means that they must be doing *something* right. Judt thought it fit to spend his waning energy reminding us all of the importance of language, to save it from becoming a free-for-all, lest ideas may also become a free-for-all without anchor in rule or standard. Language is like an ocean liner – it keeps us afloat; simply put, if language goes down, we go down with it. We should feel immensely grateful to Judt, and reward him for deepening our appreciation of what we do for a poor living.

16

Newspapers in the Classroom[34]

Quentin Crisp declared that books are for *writing*, not for *reading*. Whether he would have said the same of newspapers must remain a matter of conjecture. This little instance of *Crisperanto* should no doubt be taken as intended, with a subtle pinch of salt, for at worst it simply meant that he preferred writing to reading; at best, he might have intended something quite profound – but I shall do my very utmost to avoid profundities in everything that follows.

As for newspapers, speculation is rife concerning their future, if indeed they have a future at all. No doubt there will always be news, but will there always be news*papers*? Will the paper format be replaced entirely by online news? If so, will the news online consist of headlines and text, as at present in newspapers? Or merely of bullet points, perhaps without paragraphs, in a sort of staccato style? Or will the news be audio only – which would present difficulties for those of us who are hard of hearing? Or will there be a mixture of written text and audio 'text'? Some publishers have announced that daily papers will cease in favour of weekly publication, due to a significant fall in demand. This fall in demand is not only, or even

---

primarily, due to more stringent personal budgeting in hard times, but to the fact that more of us, almost all of us, are consulting our laptops and smartphones for news updates, partly, of course, because updates are immediate.

Perhaps the most reasonable likelihood is that newspapers, as we have come to know them, will continue to exist side by side with high-tech formats for at least the foreseeable future, in much the same way that books coexist with ebooks. Meanwhile, as teachers of English as a foreign language, we should not feel that we are stuck with the paper version, or that we are hard-done-by with hard copy.

It may seem innocuous and obvious to say that newspapers have a role to play in the classroom from good intermediate levels and upwards. And it may seem too much to say that they could, arguably, replace all, or almost all, other forms of written and reading material; yet, I am inclined to play for high stakes and assert precisely that, and I shall make the case for such an assertion if only to make a clear point yet clearer. The very least I can do is to make the case for a hobby horse of mine, namely *analytical reading* as a means of self-study and of classroom teaching.

Consider headlines. We may start from the fact that excellent headlines are almost invariably bad sentences, omitting, as they do, articles and verbs, or using verb tenses in ways that are unacceptable in sentences. 'Man sixty scales Everest' is not a sentence, and probably the first sentence in the article to which this is a well-constructed headline would read: 'A man, aged sixty, has scaled Everest'. Armed with the generally valid observation that good (i.e. well-constructed) headlines make bad sentences, students can, albeit with considerable initial help and ongoing guidance, be engaged in converting headlines into sentences. In this way they can apply the rules relating to the use of definite and indefinite articles and also practise the grammar aerobics of translating, for example, present simple into present perfect, and not forgetting the often perplexing use of *prepositions*, which are often omitted in headlines. 'Queen visits Hong Kong' becomes 'The Queen visited (has visited) Hong Kong', and 'Girl Raped in Taxi' becomes 'A girl was (has been) raped in a taxi', and this introduces simple past passive and present perfect passive into the exercise. In this way, the thorny topic of when and where we should use definite and indefinite articles can be kept constantly on the boil, while those general rules for their use which are relatively clear can be seen to apply in real, authentic, and of course sometimes tragically or cruelly authentic, applications, and the occasional exceptions to the rule can be identified and remarked upon. A daily focus on the headlines of the day becomes an exercise in grammar manipulation and a reminder that the present simple and the past participle are regularly used to replace past tense forms including their passive forms.

This kind of exercise can be used habitually, as a daily starter, so that students become gradually familiar with headlines and how to understand them. The story should, of course, shed light on the headline as much as the headline should encapsulate the story; headlines and stories are therefore complementary. Students first attempt to convert the headlines into sentences, without reading the story; they then read the story as a check on their conversions; perhaps their conversion will be discovered in the body of the text to which the headline relates. In this way, the exercise can form part of self-study and self-correction.

Or something different: give them only the photograph to which the story relates. If there's a caption, this can also be given as a clue, or it can be omitted to give their imaginations a freer rein; then the exercise consists in asking them to imagine and to write a plausible story to which the photograph/caption can relate, and also to supply a suitable headline. They are then shown the real story/caption/headline to make comparisons with what they imagined.

Or again, let them simply read the article and write down its essentials in the form bullet points resembling headlines. This will help them develop the vital skill of note-taking. Let them then convert the bullet points into sentences and paragraphs, in their own words as far as possible. They then compare their texts with the original.

In such ways, gradual and habitual exposure to newspapers will help to mitigate the trepidation with which many students approach them. Familiarity need not breed contempt; it can breed confidence, instead. Some schools have become lucky enough to receive free copies of the local or regional newspaper delivered every day. Agreed, not every teaching establishment finds itself in such a privileged position, but in the school in which I teach, students have come to expect to pick up a free copy of the local newspaper on their way to the classroom, and sometimes appear downcast when the daily issue fails to turn up. By the time I arrive, the classroom resembles the reading room of the local library, everyone silently and busily engaged in turning pages, stopping to look up a word and making a note of it in their notebooks. Too good to be true? Yes, but true nevertheless, though I would not have predicted such a degree of interest as they have come to show.

I must confess, I am proud of the fact that students now show this interest without constantly being told to do so. They are far less intimidated by the small print or by the fact that headlines often seem to strike them as gobbledegook. I allow them sufficient time to do their own scanning and note-taking, but I advise them not to become too bogged down in a lengthy article or story; and then a quick romp through some of the stories begins, with me picking out certain key but tricky lexis (e.g. 'plea' and 'squatter' in the headline 'Plea for Squatters Rights', or an idiom like 'Hats off to …' or 'explosion' as in 'Explosion in Housing', and so on; or I might ask them to convert a headline into a sentence – perhaps a similar instance to what we have done previously, so that a degree of recycling can take place.

It hardly needs to be said that lexis, comprising idioms (frequently to be met within headlines), new vocabulary, lexical collocation, an abundance of phrasal verbs, and the use of preposition-dependent adjectives, nouns and verbs, all make up the very rich linguistic tapestry of newspaper stories and articles, which is why an analysis of almost any newspaper text, chosen at random, can yields so much about the language. A teacher-led analysis can help sensitise students to this richness and help them to see what to look for and what to take careful note of in self-study reading. This may be called *analytical reading*, which is quite different from reading for gist and reading for detail in that the analysis seeks to understand the language as it is used in the expression of ideas, and not simply the ideas *per se*. The emphasis is on reading slowly and taking note of new lexis, grammar structures, prepositions, linking devices, and so on. But students should be taught how to make notes – what to look for, how sentences are put together, the molecular structure, as it were, of the atoms that are words. They should be taught quality reading and quality note-taking. A student who is taught how to read effectively is a student who is taught how to self-study effectively. It is a question of adopting the most effective learning strategy, and certainly analytical reading must be high on the list of possibilities.

Quite so. But why are newspapers of particular interest? Won't *any* text do? Newspapers are of particular interest, simply because newspapers are particularly interesting. They are *topical* and they deal with *current* events or those of the recent or immediate past. They concern the world in which we live more directly and more engagingly than a tired course-book reading text chosen simply because it satisfies the broad canons of what a reading text should look like and be about: crime, advertising, jobs, and so on; and they are chosen with a view to their broader appeal over time. In fact, on most occasions, course-book reading texts are read simply because they are *there*! True, many course book reading texts are fished out of newspapers, magazines and books of many kinds; nevertheless, they cannot have about them the immediacy of a newspaper story about what happened yesterday or a few days ago, or about what is about to happen in the very near future. Together with immediacy we must count the breadth of interest when newspapers divide into sections: fashion, jobs, cars, food, sport, health, and so on.

If the newspaper is local or regional, students have the additional advantage in reading about where they are; they have a means of finding out what went on, what goes on and what will go on, so that a newspaper is a source of entertainment news.

But as for the stories themselves, the immediacy of a story or article is more likely to inspire classroom discussion and comment. Sometimes a newspaper will follow up a story in several editions. Recently, a judge's decision in a local court case, which the class had already discussed, was commented upon critically by some members of the public, and this critical public reaction was reported in the same newspapers several days later. It was as though students could see some of their own criticisms printed back at them, providing a boost to their egos. In this way, interest in the story was sustained, and the authenticity, as it were, of their own ideas was underscored. The fact that a story is sometimes followed up in several editions can help students to follow through their own classroom discussions memorably, which is, in this instance, precisely what happened.

Newspapers are therefore catalysts of discussion and important tools in the practice of speaking skills. The *pronunciation* of useful language elements in a newspaper story is of course worth emphasising in any classroom, teacher-led, analysis of text, and these can be expected to feature in any ensuing discussion, thus affording an opportunity to repeatedly practise the items in question. The topical interest of newspaper stories is obvious, since every newspaper has its daily quota of crime, unemployment, poverty, drug abuse, etc. to relate. And since classroom discussion requires (at least, ideally) listening to others, newspapers play a role in the honing of *listening skills*. Students may also be inspired by what they have read to prepare a *presentation* to the class, offering their own views and interpretation of what they have read, in the process of practising their *speaking skills*.

The practice of *writing skills* can consist in asking students to write newspaper articles/stories of their own, complete with headlines or a letter to the editor, so that they find an interesting context in which to practise written, discursive English, the language of complaint and critical comment, the language of description, and narrative English, all with an emphasis on the orderly presentation of ideas, and with an eye to economy and precision of expression. In all this, they are clearly practising the use of past tense forms, linking devices, and suitable lexis, with a style appropriate to the function in question.

Indeed, given the skills (reading, writing, speaking and, hence, listening) that a newspaper focus can generate, together with the context it can provide for discussion of the sense and application of grammar structures and forms, and the broad window it provides into lexis of all kinds, one might be hard-put to decide what should merit primacy – course book, or newspaper! In a generous and more sensible (!) mood, we might of course simply say that at the very least they are complementary; complementarity, as distinct from substitution, is a more arguable position and one that is far less likely to offend course book writers.

Nor should we forget that we teachers should be capable of learning about the very same language we teach; and a course book can help us to focus on an aspect of the language or its application that we might otherwise have overlooked, not to mention the fact that it presents us with an order of play in our teaching, which is meant to be far less confusing than the random selection of points from a newspaper.

However, our selection need not be at all random. And this is precisely where complementarity comes in. A newspaper can help illustrate a point treated in a course book, as much as a language point in a newspaper can point teachers and students to its explication in a course book or a grammar book. It can also happen that a useful language-point in a newspaper is persistently *untreated* in course books (e.g. see my 'Identifying the Discursive Conditional', *MET*, Vol 8, No 4). The point is simply that while we are not obliged to choose between newspapers and course-books, we should recognise that the former are invaluable aids in the process of teaching and learning.

Will newspapers be completely replaced by online news sites and commentaries? Will they fade away from our breakfast tables and staff rooms in favour of portable screens? If so, will the language of newspapers change, too, so that headlines as we know them disappear also? In fact, headlines might remain and become even shorter, even cryptic – Heaven help us!

No matter, for as long as the news, topical and current comment and interest features are presented in the medium of recognisable and acceptable English, they will continue to be of invaluable use in the classroom, whatever their format might be. As matters stand at present, newspapers, although studied as a topic in their own right, as part of the topic 'The Mass Media', they are, it seems to me, a vastly underused source of current, standard written English, which offers both opportunities for students' discovery of their own potential in the language and also invaluable examples of how the language actually works.

17

Heaven Does Not Talk:
Teacher Talking Time[35]

Some very valid observations are made about Student Talking Time (STT) in Marianne Reynaud's article in Issue 75 of *English Teaching professional*. Strategies should be adopted and opportunities should be created to give maximum scope for STT in the language classroom, based on a proper appreciation of the fact that students need to know how to take advantage of such strategies and opportunities. Unless the difficulties facing the students themselves are properly understood, it is easy to understand how teachers, when faced with a sea of silence, can be afflicted with the 'disease to please' and still make no real progress towards the goal of getting their students to speak.

However, in the effort, quite right and proper, to give maximum scope to their students, teachers may find themselves troubled by an alternative disease, namely a *phobia* about talking too much, that is, a neurotic dread concerning Teacher Talking Time (TTT). It looks as though some kind of balance must be struck between STT and TTT, one which gives sufficient opportunity to students to do what they should do, namely

35   *English Teaching professional*, Issue 83, November, 2012

speak, and at the same time allows teacher to open their mouths and do what they should do, namely *teach*, and to teach in such a way that they don't end up sacrificing their personalities to the extent that they become no more than facilitating automata, for if teachers suffocate their personalities, they suffocate themselves, and then their ability to get the most out of teaching and to give of their best is seriously impaired. Facilitating automata may be the stuff of the future, but it is not a future I would ever want to be part of. It is teachers as *people* that would in such a scenario be eliminated. It is this question of *personality* that I would like to pursue a little in this article.

There are many anecdotes[36] about the Chinese teacher Confucius, a man claimed to be one of the greatest teachers the world has ever known or is ever likely to know, many of them unreliable and open to a variety of interpretations amongst scholars, and far be it from me to pretend to have more than a general reader's knowledge of the man or to query matters of translation. But one such anecdote concerns his pedagogical methods and is well worth considering here, even though we must take a *prima facie* approach to both translation and interpretation. This anecdote is based on what he considered to be an essential prerequisite of teaching, namely the silent, pervasive personality and character of the teacher. He is supposed, on one occasion, to have said: 'I would much rather not have to talk,' to which one of his disciples, Tzu-kung, responded: 'If our master did not talk, what should we disciples have to pass on?' to which Confucius then replied: 'Heaven does not speak; yet the four seasons run their course thereby. Heaven does not talk.' We are not told, but perhaps it was one of the great man's bad days; he might have exhausted himself and, finding

---

36   Smith, D.H., *Confucius*, Paladin, 1974, & Waley, A., *The Analects of Confucius*, Vintage, 1989

himself facing a sea of bewilderment, wondered whether he was really in the right job – doesn't that sound all too familiar?

It might appear that what worried Confucius should worry us, too, and that he would be quick to advocate what has been called The Silent Way. One way of pruning TTT is to cut it right back to the roots and dispense with it altogether. This may seem absurd, but it is often astonishing to what absurdities we might find ourselves reduced. But the so-called Silent Way cannot possibly be what Confucius would have endorsed, since central to what his idea of what teaching is, or should be, is the power and educating influence of the personality and character of the teacher – and it is very hard to see how primacy could be given to this by shutting teachers up altogether. Tzu-kung was quite right to remind his master that what is unexpressed cannot be passed on! And, surely, teaching is all about passing things on. We speak of charisma, and Confucius must have had it in plenty, but charisma is expressed in words. Abraham Lincoln is considered to have been one of the most charismatic of presidents, and Dr Martin Luther King one of the most charismatic of human rights activists, but if they had said little or nothing, we should not have the Gettysburg Address or the 'I have a dream' speech; and we can think of presidents and leaders who lack charisma, and in support of the allegation we allude to their inability to speak! There are actors who are said to have such a stage presence that they need hardly open their mouths to command the fullest attention of their audiences; true, but that is because they have already proved themselves in words and we know how they would sound if they *did* open their mouths. People as diverse as Ludwig Wittgenstein and Adolf Hitler had an abundance of charisma, and they needed only to walk into a room to silence the buzz of conversation; but that was due to a mixture of fear, particularly in the one case, and a surfeit of respect, particularly in the other, for many of those present were paralysed with intimidation, fearful lest relentless barbs, or insights, of one sort or another were aimed their way, losing them face, reducing them to insignificance and causing them an irreversible loss of self esteem.

Given the obvious, namely its role as a crucial means of verbal communication, a language must be expressible; its rules must be explicable and explicated, both by example and by analysis; and ex[placation and analysis cannot be rendered by an appeal either to Heaven or, for that matter, to God (remember that God is said to help only those who help themselves!) That a language teacher should talk is therefore a platitude so platitudinous that calling it such is itself platitudinous.

There can be little doubt that Confucius's pupils loved to hear him speak. He was a model of wisdom and, no doubt, his mastery of the language provided a model of how it should be spoken. They must have learned a lot simply by listening. What, of course, enthralled them was the *personality* of their teacher. Why? Because his wisdom and his mastery of the language were part and parcel of his personality and were inseparable from it! It was the personality of their teacher that they found enthralling; and it would be hard to say the same of a teacher wedded to The Silent Way. Why don't we speak of having the 'right personality' to be a teacher? Isn't this the most important requirement of all? Of course, personality is a complex concept, a kind of catch-all, and we may disagree over this or that element or over questions of degree, but patience, at least a smattering of humour, consideration and respect for others, and commitment to the task of teaching, all these would no doubt be accepted by the majority of us as fundamental requirements of good teaching. But many teachers are sadly uninspiring; the best teachers are inspiring, and you can't have inspiring teachers without personality. A teacher is inspiring because he is himself inspired; there is no other way to be genuinely inspiring. In this sense, Confucius would be right to give primacy to personality.

So, how should we rate silence? I should like to say that silence is *thin*. Think, for example, of fashion models on the catwalk. They are dangerously and lamentably thin, and they would not, I think, have suited Confucius. Yet they are revered as models of excellence. Oh dear! We really must take care lest what is dangerous and lamentable should become models of excellence in the teaching of English, or any language, or, for that matter, in the teaching of anything at all.

I remember a true model of excellence. She was an Italian teacher of Italian. If, during one of her lessons, a student should ask her a question which even remotely touched upon Italian politics, culture, history or literature, she would fly off on a tangent and talk and talk and talk, to the extent that she stood TTT on its poor head. Gone was the grammar lesson! Gone was the lesson on prepositions and Italian pronunciation! No matter, we loved to hear her speak. It was, after all, an exercise in listening comprehension, and such a welcome change from exercises in the dreaded irregularities of the *Passato Remoto* of Italian verbs. It was a listening exercise, but one without the necessity and the stress of being formally tested and graded. We were privileged to listen to how Italian should be spoken, to how native speakers do it when they do it well. We weren't slow to comment ourselves or to ask questions; and we were content with any kind of response, simple or complex, because the subjects of her verbal meanderings were difficult and we felt that we, too, were making intelligent contributions. Without having planned it, without having engineered it, she enabled her students to feel fully engaged – and all at their own pace and levels of competence. She gave us a model of excellence that was due to her inspiring personality, and it was because of this, not despite it, that her students learned Italian, because this model of excellence gave her students a target to aim at and inspired them to persevere and do better, with the phrase 'Oh, to be able to speak Italian like that!' at the forefront of their minds. She was able to inspire others like this because she was herself inspired.

What may be listed as the requirements of good teaching are there to guide and to help, not to hinder, not to suffocate; they should indeed be abstractions from what is already done, rather as the rules of grammar are extrapolations from language in use. But they must not be allowed to get in the way of good teaching, particularly *inspired* teaching – that would be a most regrettable piece of irony!

The idea that TTT imposes limitations is now almost canonical, biblically set in stone, and those who are mindful of the requirements of good teaching laid down by such august bodies as the British Council Inspectorate may be fearful of opening their mouths in the classroom lest they trespass on hallowed ground. Of course, it will do to argue, in blind defence of TTT, that Confucius himself would have endorsed it. On the contrary, the anecdote in question must be taken together with the reply of his disciple – that unless the teacher speaks, nothing will be said at all! Confucius may appeal to Heaven, but Heaven is not charged with the task of teaching English as a foreign language; we look to Heaven in vain for an analysis of verb forms and the intricacies of lexis, the explication of pronunciation rules and discourse markers. But we may well look to Heaven for the inspiration, not to say the energy, to teach.

A teacher has licence to teach, and licence should be tempered by the well-documented and well-received requirements of good teaching, to void chaos and confusion, and, simply, to avoid lessons which teach next to nothing. Likewise, these same requirements should be tempered by a little wisdom, to avoid misunderstandings about what 'good teaching' is. For it is a fallacy to suppose that strict adherence to a set of depersonalised criteria can constitute good teaching. Good teaching will pay due regard to such criteria, but only if and when such criteria can be themselves tempered by the personality of both the teacher and his class. Granted the basic need for requirements, teaching can be mechanical, lifeless and eminently forgettable – and such epithets as these remind me of the kind of 'lesson plans' that win applause from many of those who seriously believe that they can teach teachers a thing or two! Goodness knows how the progressive and incisive educationalist A.S. Neill would have coped with that, no doubt hopelessly; I can sense him turning in his grave at a rate of knots.

I recall an elderly lady who had established a school which specialised in the teaching of mathematics. She would employ people to teach with her. What about trained teachers and teacher training? 'Teacher training?' she would exclaim. 'Well, first I see whether someone *can* teach! If I see that they can teach, then and only then do I start to think about training them. More often than not, training turns out to be unnecessary, and it might even get in the way.' She was unimpressed with dossiers, personal references and academic qualifications or any kind of institutionalised gimmickry. She would see for herself, and what she looked for was something never featured amongst the criteria of good teaching, namely *personality*, and, with it and through it, the ability to put things across, to pass things on, and, above all, the ability to inspire. And if that meant her teachers occasionally talking their heads off, well so be it. Did her teachers actually succeed in teaching the children mathematics? Of course they did, and sometimes with startling results. She considered her teachers superior to the general run of traditionally trained teachers. You wouldn't dare talk to her about the limitations imposed by TTT, pointing out that TEFL is not the same as teaching mathematics. You would feel foolish in broaching the matter at all, whatever the subject being taught.

Are we wrong to talk about the requirements of good teaching, then? Not at all. But the danger is that such requirements may be seen as a total abstraction from that which gives them any life they have, in much the same way as the rules of grammar may wrongly be divorced from the real-life contexts which give birth to them. Models of teaching, however cleverly constructed and useful they may be, should never be permitted to underestimate, let alone *ignore*, the personality of the teacher nor yet the personality of the class. To bend the words of Saint Augustine, one is tempted to say 'Love teaching, and do what you will', a dictum which cleverly contains its own corrective to the chaos of wild licence, for if indeed you love teaching, it will follow that you will be mindful of TTT; you will be mindful of the requirements of good teaching *as a matter of course*; for you will impose *your own limits* from, as it were, *the inside*, rather than have them imposed from without. In general, the love of teaching imposes its own limits; but the imposition will be tempered by the personality that imposes them upon itself. Merely 'following the rules' does not a good teacher make! No external imposition can make a good teacher. It would be like saying that all you need to be a good actor is to commit your lines to memory and learn them by rote. Perverse! Some of the best lines are not learned at all, but ad-libbed. In real life, the ability to ad-lib, to make it up as you go along, seems indispensable and quite the norm. Someone might struggle to learn his lines and succeed in doing so, yet he will never make it as an actor, because something is missing – the ability to put those lines across, and they cannot be put across without something called *personality*, that wonderful, seemingly indefinable, creature which stands behind them and drives them and gives them some conviction.

Temper requirement with wisdom. Mencius tells us that Confucius abstained from extremes. To go too far is as bad as not going far enough. So much for The Silent Way, then! All the so-called requirements of good teaching should be approached with a generous degree of circumspection, for when they are too strictly applied, they are dangerous, and when they are not dangerous, they are ludicrous. What can be said about TTT can also be said about, for example, the *pace* of a lesson. Just how long *should* (what a word!) the various stages of a lesson be? Well, how long is a piece of string? How long do you *want* it to be? And can you really say in advance how long it ought to be? What right do you have to introduce 'ought' into the discussion at all? And this with no account being taken of personality whatsoever of the personality of the teacher and that of his class – as though we are applying a rule quite mechanically with no consideration of the object to be measured. Would you measure a table in the absence of the table? Or you might as well recite King Lear's storm-scene speeches as though you were reading a railway timetable out loud – All Aboard for the Storm Scene!

William James, the 19th-century American psychologist, advised teachers[37] to prepare their lessons meticulously – and then to dump all their notes into the trash-can on the way to the classroom. Heaven forbid!

---

37   James, W., *Talks to Teachers*, Harvard University Press, 1984

But then, and once again, Heaven is not charged with the task of teaching and really has nothing to say on the matter.

James recognised the importance of lesson preparation, lesson planning, timing, pace, TTT and all the rest, and I'll warrant he knew it better than our much-vaunted school inspectorates. But he also understood that all this was useless unless teachers feel comfortable with themselves; and they cannot feel comfortable with themselves unless they *are* themselves; just as actors must feel comfortable with the parts they play. (The actor Thora Hird said that for her this depended on her shoes: she had to have the right shoes for the character she was playing, and then everything else would fall into place. She worried about her lines after that, not before.)

James knew what a mess we almost invariably make of things. Even when we attempt to bring order out of chaos, we devise *requirements*, *essentials* and *criteria*, which we then seek to impose with an iron fist, forgetting that hands of iron are not the kind of hands we need when handling fine porcelain.

* * *

And now I fancy I hear a protest from all those who believe they can teach teachers a thing or two: 'Oh, but we don't seek to impose anything with a fist of iron!' Well, perhaps you don't. But you should take more care that you are not perceived to be doing so, lest you spoil many a good teacher and many a good lesson. There is something in the very notion of *requirements*, *essentials* and *criteria* that is apt to bedevil us all.

18

Analytical Reading[38]

First, definition. What is analytical reading? – not forgetting that analytical reading is not really about what we teachers can do and should do, but about what our students can be taught to do and should then do habitually by themselves. Consider the following extract[39]:

'It is easy to pay lip-service to the idea of equality for women, but in practice this is often difficult to achieve. People's attitudes do not change overnight, and it takes time, as well as education and example, to remove prejudice. In many countries, women still have great difficulty entering such professions as medicine and law, while the idea of a woman truck-driver or race-horse jockey would be unthinkable.

'In Sweden, however, equality of the sexes has been carried far. One reason for this is that there has been a shortage of labour in the country. Unemployment has been low, the population has remained static, so new jobs have had to be filled by women. Nowadays, women comprise about 40% of the working population – a high

38   *Modern English Teacher*, Vol 22, No 2, 2013
39   'Equality for Women, Sweden Shows How', George Sessler/BiltHuset

percentage compared with other countries. A second reason is that positive measures, in the form of government action, education and propaganda, have been used to bring about greater equality for women.'

Analytical reading is reading to see, to observe and *make careful written note* of such items as lexical collocation, spelling, punctuation, grammar, prepositions, phrase verbs, and last, but by no means least, idiomatic expressions and figurative language. Observation is really key here: tell students about Sherlock Holmes and remind them that his powers of deduction depend directly upon his powers of observation. To focus on just one aspect of language, lexical collocation, students can learn from the above extract that:

Equality can be *achieved/brought about/carried far*

Attitudes can *change*

Time can be *taken*

Prejudice can be *removed*

Professions can be *entered*

Ideas can be *unthinkable*

Unemployment can be *low*

Population can be *(remain) static*

Jobs can be *filled*

Measures can be *used/* can be *positive*

There can be a *shortage of population*

Population can be *working*

Difficulties can be *great*

Then there are idioms like 'to pay lip-service', 'to change overnight'. Spelling and punctuation should also be noted: the use of the hyphen in compound nouns and adjectives like 'truck-driver' and 'race-horse jockey'; how the hyphen joins words, while the dash joins *ideas*, as in '40% of the population – a high percentage compared with other countries'; and the way in which the sentence adverb 'however' is preceded by and followed by commas when it does not begin the sentence or clause to which it refers. Or there is grammar: 'there has been'/'have been used'/'have had to be filled'/'has been'/'has remained'/'would be + adjective'. And apart from these instances of *Present Perfect* and *Present Perfect Passive* forms, students may also note how the structure of 'to have difficulty' (with or without 'in') is followed by a *gerund*.

The rules and conventions of spelling and punctuation really do need to be emphasised, for the obvious reason that they differ between languages. Punctuation requires particular emphasis, especially nowadays with the increased use of *texting* from mobile and smartphones. The niceties of punctuation are seldom observed when texting; yet they are expected in examinations, and rightly so, since the observance of such rules may make the difference between sense and nonsense, or clarity and ambiguity. I shall spare the reader a litany of examples; I shall make do with the following:

1. The policeman said the boy broke the window.
2. The policeman, said the boy, broke the window.
3. The policeman, said the boy broke the window.
4. The policeman said the boy, broke the window.

In 1 the boy is clearly alleged to have broken the window; in 2 the policeman is clearly alleged to have broken the window; in 3 and 4 there is at best ambiguity, at worst nonsense.

From the short extract quoted there is a wealth of material to be gleaned by *analytical* reading. Clearly, a teacher is expected to make far more of the analysis than a student; but students should be more than capable of observing how words are used together; and even how grammar structures are used together (grammar collocation): unemployment *has been* low, and the population *has been* static, so new jobs *have had to be filled* by women (Present Perfect + Present Perfect + Present Perfect Passive).

Students are capable of identifying the grammar structures that have already been taught in lessons. Part of our job as teachers is to take the horse to the water; we should show by example what kind of things students should look for. Take, for example, the phrasal verb 'bring about' in the phrase 'to bring about greater equality for women'; it would be our job as teachers to explain the importance (currency) of this phrasal verb in discussions of *equality* and also of *change* and *development*, so that students are ready to take note of such collocations as 'bring about' a 'change'/'development', and its intransitive partner 'come about', as in 'many changes/developments have come about …'; at the same time we should point out the *preposition* 'in' that almost invariably appears in such phrases, e.g. 'many changes have come about *in* communications …' and 'many developments have been brought about *in* communications …'. In other words, we are teaching our students, *sensitising* them about the important nuts and bolts of the language, so that they know what to look for and what to take note of when they are reading alone, without the teacher at their beck and call. We are teaching them how to observe, or, better, *what kind of thing to be observant about*, so that they can take meaningful notes for themselves, and so that reading analytically becomes increasingly confident and increasingly habitual. (Incidentally, I am continually astonished at how many students, at all levels, seem never to have been taught the difference between transitive and intransitive verbs, and are therefore incapable of noting which are which in their reading, and incapable also of understanding the importance of transitivity for passive verbs forms.)

Analytical reading entails quality as distinct from quantity. Students should be encouraged to choose short texts, like short newspaper articles, and to make careful written note of new lexical items; old lexical items, too, for that matter, since a student may know the *meaning* of a familiar word but not be able to *use* it correctly, e.g. 'The police are *doing* an investigation *for* the murder', instead of 'The police are *making* an investigation *into* the murder'. The fact that they are familiar with the word 'investigation' does not guarantee their ability to use it correctly, i.e. does not guarantee a knowledge of the correct collocation; in this sense, students may well need to back track and go over old ground, lest familiarity with a word breeds a contempt for its use, expressing itself in a false assumption as to what the correct use is.

Analytical reading in small doses should become habitual; the idea is to form the habit of effective reading so that they can adopt an effective learning strategy; and the hope is that students will pick up the habit by repeated and judicious example in the classroom.

If, for example, newspapers are available, or short stories, or texts from longer stories or novels, the idea would be for the teacher to analyse sentences and paragraphs so that students know what kind of thing to look for. Children are taught the Green Cross Code for crossing roads safely: Look left, Look Right, Look left again, and if all is clear, cross. Something similar should happen when reading analytically. Read the text; look right and left of the word that is key, or the word which strikes you, even if it's a word you know already; see what prepositions/articles are used with it; if the word is a verb, notice the adverb; if the word is a noun, notice the adjective; notice the spelling; notice the use of sentence-linking devices; notice the grammar; notice the punctuation; notice the use of idioms, and phrasal verbs. Speaking here of 'the word that strikes you' may seem odd and subjective; but learners should be taught to identify key words in a sentence and then to note what surrounds them. Once again, familiarity with a word should never preclude this kind of analysis. Consider the following sentence: 'Many momentous changes have been brought about in communications by fairly recent advances in technology.' Such a sentence as this is a treasure house for note-taking (i.e. adjective, phrasal verb, and preposition for 'change', and adjective and preposition for 'advances', together with the reminder that 'advance' has a plural form whereas, as students may already have been told, its synonym 'progress' does not.)

Analytical reading is really a habit of mind. It is underpinned by a genuine desire to make progress in something difficult – or, perhaps we should say, in something *different*. If the aim is simply to use English for ordering Kentucky Fried Chicken or inquiring about the next train to King's Cross station, analytical reading may be over the top and at best surplus to requirements. But if students aim to use English for academic or professional purposes in such fields as law or medicine, or if they need it to be able to hold their own in serious debate, whether they are in the company of native speakers or not, then analytical reading is really a vital element in their studies. The ability to read analytically entails skills which put the ball firmly in the learner's court. It means that the learner can become largely autonomous and able to learn at his own pace; he becomes responsible for his own learning in that he becomes responsible for his own note-taking, selecting what seems to be of principal interest or importance.

Analytical reading is also a *catalyst*, which means that a word or phrase in a text can set the student on a journey that was not anticipated. Learning becomes more obviously a process of discovery in that the item which the learner initially wanted to look up can lead on to other items of equal or even greater interest, even to the extent that we sometimes momentarily forget what we were looking for in the first place – such is a value of a journey through a dictionary! My initial and principal purpose may be to get from Cambridge to London, but the route I opted for may take me to places of even greater interest; what is at first considered a mere stop-off can turn out to be more illuminating, more fascinating, than my original destination – hence giving a twist to R.L. Stevenson's comment that it is a better thing to travel than to arrive. And so, the text the reader begins with, and the item which spurs him towards a dictionary journey or a 'surf on the net', can be a catalyst, leading to linguistic discoveries at first undreamed of. What's new? Isn't learning a process of discovery? And how often, when approaching an issue we have never before thought of, do we discover our opinion only through discussion with others, or only through trying to write about it – in other words, without a preconception of what our own view is; and even when there are preconceptions, these can change through discussion in ways that are totally unexpected. We are merely reminding ourselves here that what we begin with is not necessarily what we end up with, and we may often be very thankful for that. Analytical reading can also allow for self-discovery, which is part of the value of learning and a forceful argument against 'an unexamined life'.

Analytical reading is an investigation to find the nuts and bolts of the language we wish to learn: how sentences are constructed, how words hang together, how grammar structures are connected, how the skeleton stands up, not forgetting the texture of spelling and punctuation; not forgetting, above all, that the skeleton is the *framework of ideas* and that ideas are the real stuff of life – things we wish to express, to criticise, to work out, to accept, reject, argue for, to argue against, to praise, to strive for. The skeleton in itself may not seem much of a living, moving thing; but it is the *precondition* of life and of movement – without it, ideas can't stand up in the first place. And, after all, if an idea is worth either supporting or knocking down, it is worth expressing correctly, for if it is not expressed correctly, it cannot be either supported or knocked down correctly, either. We must endeavour to understand something before we take up a position as either prosecuting or defending counsel – and we should encourage our students to be just as rigorous.

To give students of English, or any *other* language, some sense of the truth of all this is to offer an explanation of and a justification for analytical reading. And the expectation, or at least hope, is that once demonstrated and encouraged it will become habit-forming. To form such a habit is truly to become a *student* of the language as distinct from somebody who simply attends classes.

19

Grammar Collocation and Sentence Structure[40]

'Mitakuye oyasin' (All things are related)

Lakota Sioux Religious Precept

What follows may be seen as an attempt to answer the apparently odd question: what can the business of TEFL learn from Native American culture? It is an attempt to show that the oddity is more apparent than real.

There was a time when lexical collocation was treated as something of a novelty, a new kid on the block; not of course that anyone had *invented* it, or even *discovered* it, but what seemed to be suggested was a *focus* previously either absent or at any rate underestimated and underused. This focus provided students with a kind of *framework* of learning or study, a way of looking at words in use, that is to say words in relation to words; this was also a way in which to look at sentences and sentence construction. The acquisition of vocabulary would not now proceed *vertically*, like a shopping list, with words paraded separately without consideration for connections between language elements, but *horizontally*, which is to say in phrases and sentences made up of them – precisely the way in which they are in fact used. The words we choose have implications in terms of verbal/adverbial/adjectival/prepositional and subject/object collocation. In this sense, using the language correctly is analogous to using chess pieces correctly: the choice of a particular word has implications for how we should proceed, i.e. for future choices. No doubt due to this focus, dictionaries became more collocation sensitive, and no self-respecting 'big' dictionary would fail to include at least one sentential example of the use of the word in question; and, not to be outdone, course books provided collocation exercises and explications far more readily and explicitly than before, while teachers would take greater care to exemplify the use of words by providing sentence contexts for them on their whiteboards. 'Always ask your teacher to put the word in one or two sentences on the whiteboard' became good, matter-of-course advice to give to students who were keen on improving their vocabulary. At the same time, lexical collocation provided the stuff of further research and discussion papers, and even books. It was as though lexical collocation was a guest at a party and had been neglected for a long time but was now made the centre of attraction and given the attention he was due.

Both the existence and importance of this guest are by now taken pretty much for granted in the teaching/learning arenas of TEFL, and I shall not bore the reader by reworking the obvious, although, as in most walks of life, it is often either necessary or desirable to take a few steps back in order to take one step forward – a piece of wisdom that is indeed exemplified in the 'discovery' of the phenomenon of lexical collocation, for it was not that the 'guest' failed to turn up at the party, only that he was somehow missed.

And 'taking a step forward' might simply mean *exploiting the possibilities* of what we already know or have come more clearly to realise. Have we even begun to exploit the possibilities offered by a recognition that *things stand in relation to other things?* I very much doubt it.

For the fact is that the concept of collocation is a house of many mansions, and we should perhaps take a little time out to consider what might be called 'grammar or structural collocation'. When we turn to what we call 'grammar', which often, though not always, suggests verb tenses, we may note relations which, again like lexical collocation, have very much to do with acceptable sentence construction and therefore the *clear expression of ideas.* Students sometimes say that they understand the *meaning* of grammar items but not how to *use* them. This is analogous to saying that they understand the meaning of a word but not how to use it; and they mean that they do not understand how to use the word correctly in a *sentence*, i.e. how it goes with other words and what those other words should be. Likewise, they might understand the *mechanics* of a grammar structure, but not know how it goes with other grammar structures to make a well-formed sentence. The usefulness of grammar collocation as a tool in the teaching of sentence construction and in the comprehension of the *use* of grammar is beyond question. It is true that course book and grammar book writers pay some attention to it, and therefore also true that it is part of what we do in the classroom; but the attention paid to it is paid, as it were, by *default*, but which I mean that it is not at all *explicit*; so that whether or not students grasp instances of grammar collocation is almost a matter of chance. The impression is that what is done in books and in the classroom is ad hoc, as though grammar collocation is little more than an afterthought; and because of this, the importance and usefulness of grammar collocation is vastly *underplayed*. Like lexical collocation before it, grammar collocation comes across as a neglected guest at the party, sitting in some shadowy corner and failing to receive the respect and the attention it deserves.

I am suggesting that it should be much less ad hoc, much less of an afterthought, and much more of what we do, and that what used to be said of lexical collocation can with some justice be said of grammar collocation, namely that it should be exploited to a new level. It is really a question of attending *more explicitly* to *relations* between the components of language. Getting students to understand them is an aid to their confidence in using the language and the highroad to proficiency. Sioux 'medicine men' would habitually use the phrase 'mitakuye oyasin', broadly translatable as 'All things are related', to conclude their religious ceremonies, acknowledging in so doing the interrelatedness and interdependence of things both animate and inanimate in the natural world. Perhaps we teachers would do well to teach the phrase to acknowledge the interrelations and interdependence of the elements of language! Perhaps we still have some things to learn, perhaps things quite unexpected and unforeseen. But this much, I think, we might say with confidence, that if 'mitakuye oyasin' was and is an insight, it was one the Native Americans derived from long-standing *familiarity* with nature; they were not simply surrounded by nature; they felt themselves part of it; they did not regard themselves as *outsiders*. It was therefore eminently natural that their children should be *taught* how to see themselves and the element of which they themselves were part.

With equal confidence, we may say that a recognition of the interrelatedness and interdependence of the elements of language flows from a familiarity with our language. Familiarity may often breed contempt; but it might also breed understanding. This understanding should be conveyed to students of the language – who might then even be prompted to consider how the elements of their own, native, languages hang together. Clearly, the more we are familiar with our own language, the easier it will be to adopt the precept 'mitakuye oyasin' in connection with it; but also, the more students are taught to be aware of the phenomenon of interrelatedness, the easier it will be to construct well-formed sentences, which is to say, the easier it will be to learn the language. For this reasons students are taught, not perhaps what to read, but *how* to read, observing how the elements of the language may come together.

Some examples are in order, where we shall see *structure in relation to structure*, and *structure in relation to lexis*, this latter suggesting that words do not simply collocate with other words, but also with grammar structures:

Past Simple... Past Continuous, with 'as','when','while'; e.g. The phone
    rang while I was having a shower.

Past Simple ... Past Simple, with 'as soon as', 'when'; e.g. She spoke to
    him as soon as he arrived.

Past Simple ... Past Perfect, with 'before'; e.g. The train had already left
    before he arrived.

Present Perfect/Present Perfect Continuous, with 'It looks/seems/
    appears/sounds/as if/as though'; e.g. It sounds as though you've
    caught a cold.

Past Perfect/Past Perfect Continuous, with 'It looked, sounded/
    appeared/seemed/as if/as though'; e.g. It looked as though he had
    been running all the way.

And the following are three examples of the language of criticism and annoyance:

Present Simple ... Future Perfect, with 'By the time that'; e.g. By
the time you get home the guests will have left/ By the time world
governments take appropriate measures, the planet will/may/might
have become uninhabitable.

Past Simple ... Past Perfect, with 'By the time that'; e.g. By the time they
arrived the bus had left.

Unreal Preterite, with 'It is time/It is about time./It is high time'; e.g. It
is high time the government addressed this problem with the urgency
it deserves.

What all these examples show is the interdependence between structure
and lexis; we can see two sorts of collocation at work: structures collocate
with structures, and structures collocate with lexis. And this is no more than
to say that correct sentence structure is a happy marriage between grammar
structures and, in turn, between structures and lexis. To this extent, lexical
collocation is not merely a guide to the correct use of words, but also to the
correct use of grammar. Consider how we stress the importance of using the
right preposition for preposition-dependent words; this is lexical collocation.
But consider also how a verb used directly after a preposition must almost
invariably be a gerund; this is grammar or structural collocation. But
prepositions will not be used correctly unless these two types of collocation
are taken into account. 'I am looking forward to meet you' is an error of
grammar collocation, and it will be regarded as correct *lexical* collocation
only if 'to' is perceived to be other than what it really is, namely a preposition!

If an improved understanding of sentence structures is not to be an end in itself, we must consider precisely those contexts to which we might appeal when exemplifying them in the first place. In this respect, the protest might be 'I understand the grammar, but I don't know when to use it'; and this is a question of understanding appropriate *function*. Narrative functions best exemplify the collocation of past verb tenses, e.g. 'Scott and his party had to make the long return journey from the South Pole in the full knowledge that Amundsen had beaten them to it. That was bad enough. But as they were making their way through the snow, poor Evans fell into a hole in the ice.' And the grammar collocation of non or unreal preterit forms can be shown in a context requiring the language of criticism, perhaps in a letter of complaint, e.g. 'It is high time something was done about the state of the road outside my house. By the time the authorities take the measures required, the road will have deteriorated beyond repair.'

As teachers of English as a foreign language, we may suppose that we are in the business of teaching students *to do what we do*, which, of course, is not the same as *to think what we think*. Our business is not to tell them what to think, what to say, but to give them the tools to express their own thoughts, to teach them *how* to say what they *want* to say. That said, L2 acquisition is a process of *imitation*; we invite learners to follow our example. The extent to which they succeed in doing so constitutes the criteria of progress. To put this another way, it is not the business of students to create in L2, as though they are themselves creating the target language, but *to do as we do, to go on in the same way*. It is this business of 'going on in the same way' that is dependent on patterns, and on their following these patterns; for it is in the nature of patterns that they are repeatable.

Repeatability depends upon *relations*. If one stitch cannot be related to the next, it would hardly be possible to produce a patterned garment. If one element in a language cannot be related to another, it would not be possible to learn a language, if only because there would be no language to learn!

Language is, by its very nature, a complex of relations. We do well as teachers to point out some of these relations, and we should not be discouraged by the fact that when these relations are taken in their entirety they must inevitably produce a complicated complex; the complex as whole and at once can hardly be presented to those who are struggling to learn the language, but some of the elements or strands that make up this complex can and should be highlighted; learners do well to understand some of these strands, and they demonstrate their understanding to the extent that they are subsequently able to *go on in the same way*.

Rules depend upon relations; in fact, talking of rules and talking of relations are two ways of expressing the same thing. But when we speak of rules here, they are not rules like the rules of mathematics; the rules of mathematics admit of no exceptions; if they did they could not be rules of mathematics; the rules of language may admit of exceptions, but there is one rule that must apply, namely, *If anything goes, nothing goes.*

We readily speak of the 'rules of grammar', yet lexical collocation is no less the 'rules of words'. The rules of words are the relations between words; the rules of grammar are the relations between grammar structures, and between grammar structures and lexis.

Lexical collocation should not be taken too much for granted. It is only the tip of a very large iceberg. Grammar collocation is very much alive and requires much more attention; Icebergs are dangerous; ships founder upon them. Likewise, when students get it wrong, they are failing to understand relations. They should be taught the precept 'mitakuye oyasin' as a precept of learning. This watchword is not the end, but the beginning of linguistic wisdom.

References:

P.R.Brown, 'Lexical Collocation: A Strategy for Advanced Learners', *MET*, Vol 3, No 2, 1994 and
P.R.Brown, 'Analytical Reading', *MET*, Vol 22, No 2, 2013, both reproduced in this anthology.
John (Fire) Lame Deer and Richard Erdoes, *Lame Deer, Seeker of Visions – The Life of a Sioux Medicine Man*, Simon & Schuster.

20

The Constraints of Dogma: The Dangers of Applying Inflexible Criteria in Teaching[41]

To begin with, I feel it appropriate to make some relevant observations concerning the character of dogma.

Dogma is **simple** in that it saves us the trouble of considering alternative claimants to the throne of veracity, or of taking into account complications which tend towards the reflection that we may, after all, be only partly right, or, heaven forbid, not right at all. Complications can be dismissed as erroneous interpretations of the dogma in question. Simplicity belongs to dogma in much the way it belongs to *generalisation*; and, indeed, it is highly likely that dogma will be expressible in terms of generalisation: it is like *this*, because it is *always* like this and *must* be like this, and exceptions are erroneous. *God made the spectrum, man the pigeon holes* is not a dictum that will be taken too seriously by those under-endowed with a spirit of questioning.

Dogma is intellectually **satisfying** for those of us with limited vision in that it seems to provide us with the *essence of the matter*. We peel away the inessentials and are left with the basic, *essential truth* – forgetting that

---

the core of an apple is something we discard, or that the more an onion is peeled, the less of it we have, until, finally, we have nothing.

Dogma is **cosy**, in that in subscribing to it we become part of a group of similar subscribers, a club of exponents, all drawn together into one comfortable heap. Club members exchange ideas and compare notes; they may view with one another in the hierarchy of things; and they may differ one from another, but *never in essentials*. The basic tenets of their shared dogma are never subjected to doubt, lest they lose their slot in the batting order, or lose the respect they have earned for their unquestioning adherence to what has come to be considered obvious, namely the dogma they all share. In more sinister vein, this might also explain, at least in part, the attraction of political and religious fanaticism: fanatics enjoy the cosy, unquestioning atmosphere of quasi-philosophical discussions involving conspiracy theories of all shades of complication. Perhaps the brotherhood of man does not extend beyond the walls of these chambers of infantile discussion, but they certainly generate a 'feelgood factor' amongst the participants, who often cosily refer to each other as 'brothers'.

Dogma is **punitive**, in that it provides a neat framework in terms of which the judgement of others is possible concerning the extent to which they fail to conform to it. Those who tick all the boxes are in with a chance, while those who do not can expect the reproach of their 'betters', namely the guardians of dogma. (Reminiscent, perhaps, of the juvenile gangs that terrorise our inner cities.)

If dogma is punitive, it is also the highroad to career stability and achievement. Speak well of that which constitutes the dogma and of those who uphold it, stick to the straight and narrow, and you are likely to please those who are in a position to bestow gifts. Alternatively, kick against the traces, and the very best outcome you can expect is that you will be treated as a loose cannon, precariously poised on deck, or as an eccentric beyond the pale, but still, unaccountably, and, luckily for you, hanging on by your fingernails.

And if dogma is the foundation of career stability and achievement, it is also the soil in which **fear** is grounded: fear of doing or saying the wrong thing, for the 'wrong thing' is defined in terms of the dogma which constitutes the framework of judgement and possible punitive decision or action. 'No, not *this* way. If you go on like *this*….'. It seems a pity that the people who *care* most about 'doing the right thing' are those that *fear* the most. Perhaps it is they who should fear the least, for *caring* is the primary and principal requirement of good teaching, as it is of parenting, as it is of anything that requires sensitivity and judgement. But dogma seeks to put us all in our place, and stifles or perverts our best intentions in the process.

One thing leads to another. For if dogma breeds fear, it also fosters **insincerity**. In the field of education, a school anticipating an inspection is never the same as when it is not. A school *during* an inspection is never the same as when an inspection is not taking place. The aim is to please the inspectors; the status is not 'business as usual' during an inspection, but 'business as unusual', and this is surely a species of insincerity. It is the same when a lesson is observed: an observed lesson is very rarely business as usual.

Insincerity is a creature with groping tentacles; it not only affects paperwork and administration, but also the dynamic of both class and teacher. An inspection *stiffens* these dynamics and necessarily gives a false picture of them, the aim being always to match the false dynamic with the tenets of an inspection, i.e. with what the inspector expects to see; which is a rather incestuous form of insincerity. Neither doctors nor lawyers would tolerate this kind of insidious intrusion into their professionalism; imagine what they might say about a breach of patient and client confidentiality! But teachers offer no resistance, partly because they are not backed by powerful unions, with an aura of authority to compare with the BMA or supporting professional bodies like the Law Society. (This is an observation neither new nor original; see, for example, Neill, 1977[42]).

Examples abound from every walk of life, and they are to be found in the lives of diverse so-called 'eccentrics', from Quentin Crisp, whom some people have at last had the intelligence to elevate to the status of *social philosopher*, to A.S. Neill, whose tussles with the educational Establishment are now legendary and, we dare to hope, one day consequential. Even so, dogma continues to be alive and well, safe and sound. Where there is life, it is said, there is hope. But where there is life, *human* life, there is also error, to which hope can only ever play second fiddle.

* * *

So where, more precisely, does teaching English as a foreign language fit into this nebulous and depressing scenario?

We might begin with *insight*. However valuable, an insight should never be allowed to become a dogma. The so-called Silent Way, for example, contained useful insights into aspects of teaching methods; it was intelligent, but it was not a substitute for what teaching is or what teaching, presumably, should be, namely multi-faceted and mutable, an activity or process depending on a variety of factors: lesson type, lesson aim, class

---

42   Neill, A.S., *Neill, Neill, Orange Peel*, Quartet Books, esp. pp. 139-142

level, the personality of the class, the personalities of individual students and, last but by no means least, the personality of the teacher. There was, however, little chance that the Silent Way would become a dogma. It quickly became the butt of so many jokes, enjoyed by so many, both by its own practitioners or would-be practitioners and others, that the danger was quite otherwise, namely that any important insights it contained were in danger of being sacrificed on the altar of cynical humour. What lay at the source of such jibes was the equation, erroneous as well as ludicrous, of the Silent Way with the Silent Teacher, with all the corollaries that this equation was meant to suggest, above all the total redundancy of teachers, classrooms and schools – a kind of pedagogic nihilism. So, if humour saved the day, it did so perhaps rather too well. In the event, dogmatic anti-dogmatists like myself need not have worried.

Something can be done to mitigate such worries by the use of the word 'approach', as in the 'structural approach', the 'lexical approach' and the 'communicative approach'. Such phrases have about them more the aura of *suggestion* than of dogma. To which approaches we may add another – 'textual approach', suggesting that the teaching of grammar should grow out of a piece of text rather than consist of presentations and exercises of purely extrapolated forms, as it were *text-less*: 'Let's read this interesting article on the topic we want to discuss and let's see what grammar comes out of it,' as distinct from the structural approach: 'Let's do an exercise on the Past Perfect and then try to find a text that exemplifies it.'

It would be almost perverse to suggest that the structural and textual approaches to the teaching of grammar are mutually exclusive, that teachers should adopt the one at the expense of the other, as if to suggest that in adopting the textual approach grammar books may be dispensed with altogether. The term 'approach' here suggests *complementarity*, not exclusivity. There is neither an academic nor a practical case here for dogma. Certainly, the value, in part, of the textual approach is that it serves to remind us, in case we need reminding, that for the vast majority of students, what is of real and lasting interest is the world to which language relates and not simply the structural mechanics *per se* of the language they are striving to learn – which is not now to deny that there are students who are also genuinely interested in the language in its own right. Engineers and many non-engineers may be fascinated by how bridges are constructed; the vast majority of us, however, are more interested in crossing them to get to the other side. It is the world to which language relates and of which it is part that is the primary interest of most students, and the textual approach may help us bear that in mind. [43]

So much for approaches and methodologies. What about the criteria of good teaching? Could these be subject to dogma? It is tempting to reply: criteria that need to be applied by human beings are subject to dogma, if only because it is only such beings that can make the application, and because such beings are notorious for getting things wrong. They are notorious also for getting things partly wrong and partly right; and getting things partly wrong or partly right may be at least as bad as a clear miss, and sometimes even immeasurably worse.

We need only consider the categories in which these criteria are encrusted to be alarmed at the possibilities presented for provoking the demon of dogma. We jokingly ask, how long is a piece of string? – while sagely nodding our heads at the futility of a question asked in a vacuum. Yet, the criteria of good teaching (clear lesson aim, good lesson pace,

---

43   Brown, P. 'Lexical Collocation: A Strategy for Advanced Learners', *MET*, Vol 3, No 2, 1994

error correction, control of Teacher Talking Time, clear and appropriate board work, and so on) are often too rigidly conceived, and their practical application, or non-application, in the classroom is judged in inevitable ignorance of, not to say contempt for, the personalities of the class and of its teacher – as if to suggest that these criteria have a life of their own and are to be judged in isolation from these natural and life-giving factors. Life-giving, because it is they that will determine the length of the string, thus providing an answer to the question, not 'How long is a piece of string?' but 'How long is *this* piece of string?' It makes as much sense to say that the criteria of good teaching should be judged, *measured* as it were, in terms of the teacher and the class as it does to say that the teacher must be judged in terms of the criteria.

And this is another way of saying that criteria are intelligent if they do not degenerate into dogma; slack must be given to them and, consequently, to those who are judged in terms of them. They should function as general indicators at best. But general indicators of what? Good teaching? But a good teacher is like a good tree, and a good tree should be judged by its fruit. Well, not quite. After all, teachers are not trees, and trees need take no account of their fellows. If the teacher does not produce the result desired, it does not follow that the fault is necessarily with him, or with him alone; and if the desired result is achieved, neither does it follow that the praise should go to the teacher, or to the teacher alone.

This shows, perhaps, that whatever generalisation we may come up with may be subject to the death of a thousand cuts; and generalisations, we must remember, are all too frequently the stuff of dogma.

The reality is that no set of criteria can be infallible and no set of criteria can be infallibly *applied*. To recognise this is the beginning of wisdom.

Alas, alack, wisdom is permanently in short supply; it is a rare commodity which is perhaps becoming yet rarer. However, when infallibility is ruled out, so is dogma. The recognition of fallibility cannot exist with adherence to dogma – they are bad bedfellows.

Let's consider an example of what it might mean when the criteria of judgement are applied, or are conceived of by both observer and observed with slack or quarter being given, without consideration for the *personality of the class and of the teacher*. Teacher Talking Time (TTT) may be conceived of so rigidly as to disallow 'going off at a tangent'. The teacher may feel that telling the class an amusing anecdote ('A funny thing happened to me on the way to school this morning...') is necessarily out of place in a grammar lesson, unless, perhaps, it happens to be a lesson on, say, the Simple Past verb forms, and even then the teacher should get the students to do the job, i.e. to tell a story. Or, what about showing the students a musical masterclass given by the cellist Paul Tortelier? Is this ruled out, too? Of course, you might do this to illustrate the idioms 'You should go for it' and 'You should let yourself go', which the great man tells the young cellist sitting nervously in front of him. Maybe it's a speaking lesson, and you want your students to loosen up and not be too afraid of making mistakes. But does the criterion 'lesson pace' allow you to go off on a tangent? Do you feel *permitted* to go off on a tangent?

You might show your students a clip or two from one of Tortelier's masterclasses simply because you want your students to know about Tortelier and to hear him speak and play; with any luck they might follow this up in their own time. Here, as the teacher, you are fishing – and hoping for a catch; after all, you are introducing them to the world to which the language relates, and in this instance to an aspect of the world which they might not know. Tortelier speaks English; your students may listen to him again, and they too may be inspired, as the young cellist was, and they may loosen up and let themselves go, speaking English or playing maracas, no matter! Why did you choose Tortelier? Because he just came into your mind, there and then! And perhaps because you too were impressed, perhaps even inspired, by the man. This might help us to understand what kind of person you, the teacher, are – when we know what impresses you and what you hope might impress some, if not all, your students, too. Of course, you might know that one of your students is learning to play the cello, and that another plays piano; in catering for your own likes, you are catering for theirs also. And for those who prefer heavy metal? Well, they might as well at least glimpse the other side of the Great Divide.

Going off at a tangent can be importantly informative, profoundly inspirational and catalytic, vastly entertaining, or simply great fun, and not entirely disconnected with the lesson. And what is more, indeed precisely for these reasons, it may be the most memorable part of the whole lesson.

Yes, that's all very well. But what about the *main thrust* of the lesson *itself*? What about 'lesson aim'?

What a silly question! As if to suggest that achieving an aim is incompatible with achieving a bit of slack! In fact, going off at a tangent may help to make 'the main thrust' of the lesson more memorable, such that far from being compromised, the main point of the lesson has been *enhanced*.

Name-dropping is a good example of 'going off at a tangent'. If you happen to be teaching in Cambridge, ask your students what they can find out about John Milton, Oliver Cromwell, Watson and Crick, Stephen Hawking, Bertrand Russell … the list goes on and on. Getting your students to think about where they are and how it relates to other places and times and people is an interesting challenge. Every city can boast something of interest. What a pity that students should remain ignorant. (Without its great names, history and architecture, Cambridge would be as dull as a deserted seaside guesthouse in midwinter.) This is the kind of challenge that can come at the drop of a hat, generating reading, note-taking and speaking practice, not to mention developing an interest in matters other than the language *per se*, matters that, in turn, can help students to improve their English and inspire them to do better still. Which name do you drop at a particular time? That depends on who comes to mind, which, in turn, usually depends on the text you are looking at, or on the illustrative sentence you have just written on the whiteboard. There are many different prompts for name-dropping, and none of them are decided in advance.

If, on the other hand, you happen to believe that TTT is a disease more to be feared than the Black Death, you might find yourself ruling out 'inessential material', which would include tangential excursions. With one swift and callous stroke of the 'criterion scalpel' you will remove your own personal likes and dislikes and the prompts that go with them, consigning them to the trash can, and in doing so expel your personality from the classroom as though it were a most unwelcome guest. You will also ignore the fact that your students need to know something about where they are, or that one of your students is a budding cellist, another a pianist, or that they should 'Let themselves go' and loosen up, like Tortelier's pupil, in their speaking lessons. Such tangential excursions emanate from your personality, not from the pages of a course book or a grammar book; and that personality expresses itself, and indeed can grow, in reaction to the personality of your class.

So what are we to say?

We *might* say that the phenomenon of good teaching is at best a *variable constant*, variable because the categories of assessment which are normally applied must themselves be tempered by a consideration of the personalities of the class and its teacher, and personalities are variable, perhaps from one day to the next, possibly from one lesson to the next, much depending on moods and the aspirations of the day, and on student intake or turnover, which can fluctuate daily. The phrase 'variable constant' will not of course do for those who shy away from contradiction. But at least the phrase has about it an air of paradox, and the virtue of extricating us feet-first from the murky and suffocating wells of dogma into waters which are equally murky but rather less suffocating and therefore more palatable, since they provide a measure of slack to the usual application of the criteria of assessment in teaching. Or shall we say, instead, that good teaching is a nebulous constant, because talk of lesson aim, lesson pace, TTT, board work, error correction etc. is a classification that attempts to render this nebulous constant more comprehensible and assessable – which is all very well, provided we do not forget what it is that renders this constant *nebulous*, namely the essential and mutable phenomenon of *personality*.

The items listed in the classification are aspects of teaching, not the whole of teaching; the list is as noteworthy for what it leaves out as for what it contains, in much the same way that language is not all *grammar*, nor all *lexis*; the fact that we teach language in parts may be misleading; for language is far greater than the sum of its parts. Likewise, the classification we are discussing fails to take into account the *dynamic* of the class, for this is another way of talking about the personality of the class; in a sense, inspection, in terms of this classification, *must necessarily* omit the dynamic of the class observed, if only because inspection *changes* that dynamic – much in the way that the warm waters of summer are iced over in hard winters. Inspection implies observation, and observation alters the dynamic of that which is observed. The *knowledge* that you are being observed alters the character of that dynamic. The same cannot be said, incidentally, of trees.

Why bother with inspections at all? Neill seemed to suggest that they might be dispensed with altogether. He is not of course taking into account that the application of the Commercial Principle is heavily at work, especially in the field of private education. A private language school is of course a business, and must survive as one. A badge of recognition is good for business, and whatever is good for business must be pursued; anything less would seem irrational. Recognition is expected to attract customers or clients, or, as teachers prefer to call them, students. We begin with the premise of recognition: ergo inspection, ergo assessment, ergo criteria – and ergo the dangers of dogma, that is, of refusing to see that good teaching is, has always been, and hopefully will always be, a variable constant.

We are bound to acknowledge that very few teachers teach well *all* of the time, and that *most* of us teach well *some* of the time, and that *no* teacher teaches badly *all* of the time. It is just as hard to imagine a teacher teaching badly all of the time as it is to imagine one who teaches superlatively all of the time. Now *these* are variables for you! It seems to follow, therefore, that there are occasions when a good teacher could do better (incidentally, a good teacher will be perfectly well aware of them) and that these failings should be addressed.

Isn't this a solid case, then, for school inspections? And, after all, it's not as though medicine and law are bereft of watchdog organisations with criteria of judgement and punitive powers. Should we not admit, then, that inspections are a *necessary evil?* But this is yet another phrase that gets the grey cells tingling. It is precisely those of us, and our number is legion, who are subject to the excesses of dogma, who can be expected to sit easy with the idea that an evil must be necessary. Expel personality from a class of students and you are left with something else; divorce personality from the teacher, and you have no teacher, no *human* version, anyway. The personality of the class and that of the teacher, and the interplay between the two, are nebulous factors but no less real for that; and what is nebulous defies measurement. Therefore, if factored into the usual list of good teaching criteria, questions of personality inevitably muddy the waters of assessment and render the standard criteria at best unreliable, at worst irrelevant. In terms of the criteria strictly conceived and applied, it is infinitely easier to see both teachers and the students they teach as *automata.*

Therefore, questions of personality are *not* factored in. Because they are not factored in, we are left with the dogma of soulless criteria. This is the 'evil' in the 'necessary evil' of formal assessment.

21

'Demand High'?: A Critical Postscript[44]

I was interested to read Phil Keegan's keynote article ('Deliberate Practice and High Expectations') in April's issue of *MET*. It is refreshing to be reminded that while we should endeavour to make our lessons enjoyable and entertaining, we should also remember *to teach something*. This comment is not intended to strike a note of sarcasm. To say that student motivation has something to do with enabling students to see that they are making progress towards their linguistic goals is, if a platitude, one worth stating. Challenging students according to their capabilities is what makes this progress a real possibility. So far, so good.

But then, Keegan is anxious to inform us that 'demanding more from students does not mean focusing on accuracy and correct forms'. He does not recommend 'returning to the bad old days of audio-lingualism and grammar/translation'. Why? Presumably because: 'Successful communication and deeper understanding and awareness of the language is key.'

Now here, I confess, I am at a loss, and must therefore take issue.

True, demanding more from students does not *only* mean focusing on accuracy and correct forms; it may not mean this at all if the problem is

---

a lack of self-esteem and a lack of self-confidence; in such a case, a focus on accuracy and correct forms may compound the problem and, if pushed too far, even render it insoluble. Fear of getting things wrong may issue in nothing being written or spoken at all. We may be reminded here of what, in psychiatric circles, is known as 'purpose tremor': for example, trying to thread a needle without pressure and when you have all the time in the world to do it is easier than when you are stuck for time and someone is telling you to get a move on; your hand begins to shake and the thought that you may mess it up causes you to do precisely that. When the idea of 'purpose' is strong, the tendency towards error is more likely and more pronounced. The problem is also akin to 'trying too hard': the more conscious we are of the importance of avoiding errors, the more errors we seem to make. The problem of 'purpose tremors' is widespread, from threading needles under pressure to speaking in public in L1, let alone L2. 'Unaccustomed as I am to addressing people in public…' is a let-out clause for the errors anticipated by having to speak under pressure and is itself an expression of stress.

'I don't like these cold, precise, perfect people, who, in order not to speak wrong, never speak at all, and in order not to do wrong, never do anything,' said Henry Ward Beecher.

And perhaps nowhere is this reluctance to speak so marked, so understandable and so ironically unfortunate than in the language classroom, in lessons which are precisely aimed to enable students to practise speaking in L2. Students certainly *want* to speak, but they are too reluctant to *give things a go*.

We teachers should therefore encourage our students to relax and not be overly concerned about making errors; we are there to correct, and even correction should be done with sensitivity and a measure of allowance, taking a host of personal, cultural and linguistic factors into account. There is such a thing as *over*-correction. We might tell our students that it is better to make a mistake in the classroom than in the 'real world' or the 'world outside', where errors might have more serious or embarrassing consequences; better to err amongst friends and peers than in the colder circles of the 'outside world'; besides, the errors they make are not at all shameful but a natural part of the process of learning; in fact, mistakes are welcome, because they provide work for teachers; without them, we should all be redundant. This is the kind of stuff we might tell our students. Even so, 'giving things a go' means 'letting go', and this is usually much easier said than done.

All this is right and proper. The whole idea is to get students to speak or to put pen to paper, not to shut them up for fear of making mistakes. Simply, if they are too conscious of making errors, they will produce nothing, and, as King Lear says: 'Nothing will come of nothing.'

What we need is for students to produce *something* so that something will come of something. But now the question is: What is the *something* that we hope will come from the something which students themselves produce? This question is connected with the fact, and hopefully it is *an acknowledged fact*, that teachers should correct the errors students make. If there is such a thing as over-correction, there is also such a thing as *under*-correction. Or are we really to say that mistakes are really neither here nor there? And would students themselves be happy to hear us say that?

Keegan says: 'Communication and deeper understanding and awareness of the language are key.' There can be no serious disagreement here, either. But then, communication, deeper understanding and awareness of the language is related, and *logically* related at that, to accuracy and correct forms that we might well feel a little silly in having to state the fact at all.

We do not expect total accuracy and correct forms from those struggling to learn the language; but we do expect *a gradual progression towards* accuracy and correct forms so that students will be able to communicate their ideas accurately and correctly and avoid misunderstandings and embarrassment or, for that matter, total communication failure. *Per parlare sai parlare* is an Italian aphorism reminding us that it is through speaking that we learn to speak. But the idea here is that it is from the inaccuracies and incorrect forms we produce, we learn, through correction, precisely what the accurate and correct forms *are!* 'Accuracy and correct forms' is the *something* that should come from the something that we attempt to express in L2 albeit inaccurately and incorrectly.

If the idea is that we should give our students a good bit of slack and not demand from them the strictest forms of accuracy before they have had a chance to get things wrong, there can be little dispute. After all, it is often asking too much of native speakers to produce their own language strictly according to the canons of correct grammatical and lexical form, a fact that prompted that cynical remark from G.B. Shaw that the English are the only people in the world who cannot speak their own language. Shaw's natural cynicism got the better of him, as it so often did; how many amongst the Spanish speak perfect Spanish, how many amongst the French speak perfect French, how many amongst the Japanese speak perfect Japanese…?! As for the British, the majority, it might not be too bold to say, would struggle with many of the questions posed in the Cambridge Examinations, especially the Advanced and Proficiency Examinations.

We should not therefore expect our students to run before they can walk. It follows that, commensurate with their stages of development, we should not expect from them much more than they are *capable* of giving at any given stage.

Well, this is one thing. But it is quite another to say that 'demanding more from students does not mean focusing on accuracy and correct forms', as if to suggest that accuracy and correct forms form *no* part of the picture at all. In fact, one would have thought that it is precisely 'accuracy and correct forms' that can enable us to get the best out of so-called 'demand high' teaching, because, in demand-high teaching, we, as teachers, should always be attempting to *push the boundaries*, and we should be encouraging our students to do likewise. This is what the *challenge* of learning a foreign language is all about. It is just this that 'successful communication and deeper understanding and awareness of the language' inevitably (logically!) *requires*! Let's clarify this further.

Challenge involves pushing the boundaries. And pushing the boundaries is connected with the attempt to express clearly and accurately what one thinks and feels, and with the ability to understand clearly and accurately what others think and feel. And it is precisely this that I have understood *communication*, and therefore *language*, to be all about. It is to *this* end that the focus on accuracy and correct forms should be pursued, not for some foppish and prudish regard for standards and correctness. We should not confuse 'accuracy and correct forms' with aristocratic table manners, the etiquette of the Victorian dining room, the kind of rules which, no doubt for a large part of the time, get in the way of genuine communication. Our *linguistic* standards are there, not as a hindrance to communication, but precisely to enable communication of thought and feeling to take place at all. Push the boundaries towards accuracy and correct forms and, with effort, you may get somewhere; this constitutes the *challenge*. But if you push the boundaries in the opposite direction by claiming, or at least seeming to claim, that accuracy and correct forms are of little importance, if you treat them as many of us have come to treat the social norms of Victorian aristocracy, you are very close to saying that anything goes; and we should know that that can't be right, because *if anything goes, nothing goes*; we are back to nothing again, which is where we do not want to be, and where our students do not want to be, either, since it is a place which makes nonsense of language, of *any* language, of language *per se*. We are back to the jungle, swinging from tree to tree, making the occasional inarticulate grunt; or perhaps we are on the road to 'doublespeak' and an Orwellian future, one in which language is simplified to nothing, stripped down to its bare essentials, rendering the kind of 'depth' and 'understanding' and 'awareness' to which Keegan alludes impossible and therefore non-existent.

This is why the derogatory reference to the 'bad old days of audio-lingualism and grammar/translation' is somewhat perplexing and not a little worrying. This can't of course mean that grammar is unimportant. Perhaps the idea is that translation exercises are an irrelevance and a waste of time. (Oh, dear!) If so, it is hard to see how anyone managed to learn a foreign language at all in the 'bad old days' – what a wonder that they did! And yet, of course, people did learn foreign languages; not only did they learn them, but they learned, admittedly in a variety of ways, to speak and to write them fluently and accurately, every bit as much as people learn them now, and perhaps better, sometimes even *much* better.

One might have thought that a translation exercise is a surefire way of helping us to learn how L2 works in relation to L1; to say nothing of learning much better how L1 works *per se*, i.e. by enabling us to get a deeper understanding of our *own* language, of the language in a passage we translate into L2. (Compare: if you want to know your own country better, leave it, and go and live in another.) *Suppose* you come across something that interests you in your reading in L1; it would be natural to ask how this might be rendered in L2; you might be sufficiently motivated, even inspired, by a text in L1 to try to translate it into L2, or of course *vice versa*. How can translation be a bad thing?

In my own experience, an Italian student was so struck by a sentence he had come across in Tolkien's *The Lord of the Rings*[45] that we was motivated to see how it would come out in Italian: 'The world is indeed full of peril, and in it there are many dark places; but still there is much that is fair, and though in all lands love is now mingled with grief, it grows perhaps the greater.'

He concluded that it did not come out so well in Italian, but several attempts to come close did him a great deal of good; he learned a little more about English, and a little more about Italian, too.

If the derogatory reference to translation, to accuracy and correct forms is nothing more than an attack upon obsession, such that the willingness to 'have a go' is sacrificed on the altar of fear of getting things wrong, so be it. But the answer to this is to help students to relax and to understand the truth in the aphorism *per parlare sai parlare*, and to understand that there is no indignity in learning to crawl before one learns to walk, in learning to walk before one can run, in learning to sit up before one can stand up.

It is to be seriously doubted whether any kind of obsession is without very serious flaws; even an obsession always to tell the truth, or an obsession to see justice always done. But this does not mean that truth and justice are of little account, still less that they are of no account at all.

---

45   *The Fellowship of the Ring*, Chapter 6

Likewise, the case against the obsession 'always to get things right' does not imply that 'getting things right' is unimportant – that would be like throwing the baby out with the bathwater, just as it would if 'accuracy and correct forms' were sacrificed for the sake of so-called 'communication'. Communication is *what*, we are bound to ask? It would not be a case for 'demand-high' teaching, but 'demand-low' teaching, or, as *logic* demands, 'demand-nothing' teaching.

And what exactly is 'auto-lingualism'? Does it mean repetition of linguistic models uttered by the teacher or electronically? Does it refer to drills? Learning a language well is obviously a question of the ability to reproduce the language as native speakers produce it; the extent to which a non-native speaker is able to reproduce forms to an established or conventional norm, the better he is said to have learned the language. Correct pronunciation and sentence structure, correct lexical collocation and the correct use of idioms and prepositions are all in *the mix* of what is regarded as 'the norm'. Much of this is learned parrot fashion; it *has* to be, in the sense that learners cannot devise their own rules, their own 'norms'. And we would be hard put to explain much of what we teach other than by saying: 'Well, this is how we do it, and that's that.'

There are those who decry students reading out loud from a text. I am not amongst them. I hold no strong or compelling brief in favour of doing so; but neither do I hold any strong or compelling brief against it. To me, it seems one of the most reasonable things to ask a student to do. True, it may sometimes be too much to approach this exercise 'cold', at first glance, and pre-reading by the teacher, with some analysis, may be desirable. However it is done, in the process students achieve some working models of correct sound structures: syllable stress, intonation, and so on. Similarly, drilling is sometimes a good idea, even at advanced levels; and again, it would be done to give an idea of standard forms or sound patterns. So, why knock drilling? Or, rather, *why go out of one's way* to knock it? Students usually like it, perhaps because they find it reassuring, or because they feel they need it, or, simply, because they expect it; and perhaps this alone suggests that the activity is sufficiently valid.

In the absence of such 'models' of 'accuracy and correct forms', so-called 'demand-high' teaching would seem to be a bridge too far – or no bridge at all! Without them, what on earth could possibly be *demanded?*

22

Chess, Wardrobes and Pizza: Analogical Models[46]

How important features of language are presented to students will determine how they are perceived. Some perceptions, we might call some of them 'mental pictures', are more useful than others, and their usefulness lies in the fact that they can help provide a framework of approach to language-learning which may facilitate the process or, at any rate, make the journey of L2 acquisition more manageable – even perhaps enjoyable. These 'mental pictures' may be formed through the construction of analogy and, although we might relish the retort that 'analogies are odious', we can usually get some mileage out of them; they can play a positive role in and out of the classroom. Some examples should illustrate the point.

Analogy 1: Chess

In chess, we must understand the capability of each piece in the game, which means understanding how each piece can move, what it can and cannot do according to the rules which govern it. Understanding the capability of the pieces in chess is understanding what they *mean*. This

---

46   *English Teaching professional*, Issue 96, January 2015

is basic to using the pieces at all. If we don't know what you can do with them, the moves they can make, we can't even start to play the game. And knowing the meaning of your pieces implies knowing the meaning of your opponent's pieces, too.

Then, assuming that you know the meaning of each piece on the board, moving a piece *well* does not mean moving it in isolation, that is, in total disregard to the disposition of your opponent's pieces. In a serious game of chess, once you touch a chess piece you are obliged to move it, and whether or not your move is judged to be *sensible* will depend on how well you have taken into account the relation of the piece in question to the others on the board, 'others' meaning both your own and your opponent's.

It is of course possible to know what each piece *means*, and still play badly. 'He learned all the rules, but he never played well' is not at all contradictory. Had he not learned all the rules he would not have been capable of playing at all! He had learned the meaning of all the chess pieces, but he never managed to move them well enough to defeat his opponent.

Link to language (collocation: lexical and grammatical)

It is also possible to know the meaning of a *word*, and how to pronounce it and how to spell it, and still use it badly. Using words correctly, like playing chess well, requires more than simply knowing what they mean; it requires knowledge of how they stand *in relation to* other words. No-one makes a move in chess without first taking into account the disposition of all the pieces on the board, both his own and his opponent's – unless, that is, he is determined to lose the game. Likewise, if, for example, you choose to use the word 'promise', you might find yourself in difficulties if you don't know that we 'make', 'keep' and 'break' promises; or, if you choose the word 'strategy', you do not know that strategies are 'devised', 'adopted' and 'implemented'.

True, you just might manage to get through the chess game, just as when we muddle through a speech after a series of embarrassing stammers, because we don't know the subject sufficiently well and have just hoped for the best. We get through the speech, but without applause, or with only grudging applause. 'Hoping for the best' does not inspire us with much confidence, and a lack of confidence is something we can well do without. 'Never again,' we mutter to ourselves, as the speech comes to a dishonourable end. In chess, 'muddling through' is unlikely to mean playing intelligently, much less winning. Similarly, a student's use of the words 'promise' and 'strategy' are unlikely to attract the merit they would otherwise deserve especially if they are *key* words and he does not know what words collocate with them; he might succeed in making himself understood, in 'communicating' his ideas, albeit roughly; but he is unlikely to be complimented on his English; and depending on the complexity of the ideas he wishes to express, he might well have failed to 'communicate' precisely what he meant. He has 'muddled through'; but his confidence may well have taken a battering. For confidence is nourished by knowledge and shaken by ignorance.

What goes for lexis also goes for grammar. Understanding a grammar structure involves more than simply understanding its mechanical construction, its component parts. It means knowing how to *use* it correctly, knowing what to *do* with it. It means knowing, for example, that the *Past Simple* is frequently to be found with the *Past Continuous*, as in: 'I was tucking into a steak when she arrived out of the blue'; or that the *Present Perfect* frequently appears in explanation of a fact expressible in the *Present Simple*, as in: 'He's shattered. He's just finished digging the vegetable patch.'

Note also the frequency of the word 'just' in many similar examples. So, what we call 'collocation' is a pattern of relations between words, between grammar structures, and between words and grammar structures.

A language is vastly more complicated than a game of chess. Improving your knowledge of vocabulary does not simply mean endlessly adding items to a list, like a vertical shopping list of individual items. We don't use words 'vertically', but 'horizontally', which means left-to-right in *sentences*. Improving your knowledge of vocabulary means using words 'horizontally' in such a way that does full and proper justice to the words in question. I do not do justice to the word 'promise' if I say 'She always does promises which she never holds'(?), or to the word 'strategy', if I complain that the government has 'taken a strategy which is hard to do'. We should do justice to the language we are learning, which means that we should make every effort to use it *correctly*. If what you want to say doesn't come out right, then how do I know what you want to say?

And that is the challenge that defines so-called 'demand-high learning'. A good game of chess can be played just for fun – fun is what chess should be all about, anyway – but few people would bother to play it at all if it involved little or no challenge. A competent chess player is not expected to get much fun out of a game with a beginner, because the better a player is the more he relishes challenge. Experts need to feel challenged, otherwise there's not much point in being an expert at all.

Analogy 2: Wardrobes

Wardrobes contain clothes, and there are clothes for different occasions: party dresses and pin-striped suits are not for gardening; beachwear is not for job interviews. Wearing jeans to a funeral may be taken as a mark of disrespect; black top hat and tails on a picnic is, to say the very least, eccentric, though personally I'm all for a generous touch of eccentricity, when it is genuine and not posturing; but eccentricity does not sit well with everyone and on all occasions. A cellist once said that he would never play Bach, either for himself alone or to an audience, unless he was dressed formally in black, because, he said, he wanted to show the utmost respect to the composer; I find that sentiment understandable and acceptable, though perhaps not everyone would – no doubt it depends on how you feel about Bach!

Clothes generally say something about the occasion on which they are worn and about those who wear them. Quentin Crisp once said that clothes should show the world who (what?) you are, or at any rate who (what?) you *think* you are. But, granting the importance of eccentricity and individual style, 'horses for courses' is a widely acceptable principle. So much so that should someone turn up in the 'wrong' clothes, one may be forgiven for thinking that he has mistaken the occasion, or the game: 'I'm terribly sorry – I didn't know we were going to a funeral!' he stammered, as he quickly kicked off his football boots and stuffed them back into his duffle bag. And after turning up at the bank in her pink, polka-dot pyjamas, her failure to win hearts and minds during the interview and get the job as branch manager was a foregone conclusion. Your failure to wear the 'right' clothes for a job at the bank will go against you, unless, of course, you have sufficiently redeeming qualities; and unless the bank is exceptionally enlightened, which, in the general run of things, banks are decidedly not.

Link to language: social register

The choice between formal and informal English, commonly referred to as 'social register', depends on the occasion and the kind of game one wishes to play. The use of formal English on occasions which require informality might suggest, if not eccentricity, then an air of superiority or of 'pulling rank', while informality on occasions which require formality may suggest disrespect and antagonism. A letter of application for a job or university placement might not suggest sincerity if it is written in 'street language', and the more perfect, authentic, the street language is, the greater the degree of insincerity, which is why an answer to an examination question requiring formal register might be written in perfect street language from start to finish and yet fail outright to satisfy the examination requirement. We might tell a student, 'No you really can't address the university admissions officer as "Hey, man!" – though I applaud the fact that you know that this kind of address exists.'

Writers like Charles Dickens found occasion for humour in the fact that social registers can be confused one with the other. His creation Mr Micawber, in *David Copperfield*, is a good example – but while this character is a brilliant literary invention and makes us rock with laughter, his verbosity and feigned formality would be insufferable in real life, tolerable only in very small doses and when the humorous intention was explicit and transitory: '"Copperfield," said Mr Micawber, "farewell! Every happiness and prosperity! If in the progress of revolving years, I could persuade myself that my blighted destiny had been a warning to you, I should feel that I had not occupied another man's place in existence altogether in vain. In case of anything turning up (of which I am rather confident), I shall be extremely happy if it should be in my power to improve your prospects."'

As is so often the case, in Dickens and elsewhere, humour is humour by default, the cross-wiring of place, or time, or person. Concerning social register, the effect is wonderful and we love both Micawber and his creator, but it would be a poor strategy for those who wish to perform well in examinations in English as a Foreign Language.

Analogy 3: Pizza

Making a good pizza, like making a good anything else, depends on using the right ingredients. That's why we have recipes and recipe books. The *combination* and *quality* of those ingredients will determine whether the outcome is a triumph, a flop, or just passable. Strawberries with fish as a pizza topping just may inspire us to question convention, and we may even get away with it sometimes and with some judges, but we are unlikely to make many culinary friends. Better to stick to the highways, and leave the byways to those who have absolutely nothing to lose, least of all a good reputation.

The ability to recognise the right ingredients and to choose only those of quality seems to be a prerequisite of good cooking. This is connected with good taste, and good taste in cooking, as in music, is connected with judgement; and judgement is connected with style. Style, not in the flamboyant sense of mere presentation or 'posturing', but in the *quality of outcome*.

Link to language: academic style

The use of sentence-linking devices like 'however' and 'despite', and the different punctuation patterns that such devices require in writing, the careful use of paragraphing, the attention that must be paid to spelling, especially the spelling of key words, and the especial attention that must be paid to lexical collocation – all this, and more, makes up what we may roughly call *academic style*.

This is the style that should bring to mind the concepts 'intellectual honesty' and 'academic integrity', two phrases which are themselves important instances of lexical collocation. It is a style that should be partnered with quality cuisine as distinct from junk food. It is the linguistic equivalent of high cuisine. There is no room here for your just-average fish 'n'chips. It is the difference between something, *anything*, to pacify your taste buds after a couple of pints of beer, and something vastly important to say to your stomach.

We should hasten to add that style is not to be confused with substance; all style and no substance will not do; but then, it is not so easy to put it the other way round: 'all substance and no style' does not seem nearly so plausible.

* * *

Presenting language, or aspects of language, analogically, is an attempt to make language acquisition a more appealing, hopefully more comprehensible, way of spending our very precious time. In my own teaching experience, students have found it useful to look at different aspects of language in these different ways. Usefulness is everything; when such devices cease to be useful they may be more usefully discarded.

Contents

BV - #0075 - 011124 - C0 - 234/156/11 - PB - 9781780916590 - Gloss Lamination